Essex

The World's Wackiest

SPANISH JOKE BOOK

500 Puns Guaranteed to Drive You Across the Río Groan-de!

SUE FENTON

D0168561

New York   Chicago   San Francisco   Lisbon   London   Madrid   Mexico City
Milan   New Delhi   San Juan   Seoul   Singapore   Sydney   Toronto

Library of Congress Cataloging-in-Publication Data

Fenton, Sue.
    The world's wackiest Spanish joke book : 500 puns guaranteed to drive
you across the Rio Groan-de! / Sue Fenton.
        p.   cm.
    ISBN 0-07-147901-5
    1. Puns and punning.   2. Spanish language—Humor.

PN6231.P8 F46   2006
468.102/07—dc22   2006048110

1 2 3 4 5 6 7 8 9 10 11 12 13 14 15 16 17 18 19   FGR/FGR   0 9 8 7 6

ISBN-13: 978-0-07-147901-1
ISBN-10:   0-07-147901-5

Interior design by Think Design Group, LLC
Interior artwork by Luc Nisset

McGraw-Hill books are available at special quantity discounts to use as premiums
and sales promotions, or for use in corporate training programs. For more
information, please write to the Director of Special Sales, Professional Publishing,
McGraw-Hill, Two Penn Plaza, New York, NY 10121-2298. Or contact your local
bookstore.

This book is printed on acid-free paper.

This book is dedicated to my loving family, my wonderful friends, and to the playful spirit in all of us.

¡HOLA!

Welcome to this "puñata" of 500 jokes . . . with a Spanish twist! It's a celebration of the beautiful Spanish language, and you're invited to join the fiesta of fun.

The jokes are asked in English and the answers playfully fracture Spanish and warp pronunciations. There is also a big dose of "Spanglish"—words that mix Spanish and English. The jokes are sprinkled with pop culture confetti from Mexico to Spain. From Harry Potter, to Oreos, iPods, Fruit of the Loom, to chile peppers—anything goes!

Some of the jokes are based on America's general awareness of Spanish and the Spanish-speaking world. Others require some knowledge of Spanish, but if you get stumped there are vocabulary notes to help you. While your mind is being challenged and teased, you can dust off your Spanish or learn some more Spanish, and find out some trivia about the Spanish-speaking world at the same time.

Now it's time to get "muy loco, ¿comprende?" Put on a CD of salsa, flamenco, or reggaetón music. Break open a bag of tortilla chips and get some salsa. Then relax and let yourself go. Expect the unexpected as you cross the "Río Groande." May you chuckle with a Spanish accent. Soon you will be able to say . . .

¡HABLO ES-PUÑ-OL!

Did You Know That Spanish . . .

- is the first language of 330 million people in the world and the second language of 100 million people for a total of more than 400 million speakers?

- is the official language of twenty-one countries?

- is tied with English for the second most spoken language in the world after Chinese?

- is an official language of the United Nations?

- is spoken by thirty million Americans or 12 percent of the population of the United States?

- is spoken by so many people in the United States that it is the fifth largest Spanish-speaking country in the world?

- is the most common second language studied in schools?

- is spoken by so many people in Los Angeles that it's the second largest Spanish-speaking city in the world?

¡OLÉ MOLE!

SAY WHAT?

Here are some pronunciation tips to help you pronounce any new Spanish words.

Vowels

a	AAH	m<u>a</u>ma
e	EH	<u>e</u>lephant
i	EE	p<u>i</u>zza
o	OH	cl<u>o</u>se
u	OO	sham<u>poo</u>

Common Vowel Combinations

ai, ay	UH-EE	motor<u>cy</u>cle
au	AH-OO	<u>Ou</u>ch!
ei, ey	AY	Ok<u>ay</u>!
oi, oy	OY	t<u>oy</u>

Consonants

Spanish consonants sound like English ones, with these considerations:

b, v	B	<u>b</u>aseball
c + a, o, u	K	<u>c</u>omedy
c + e, i	SS, TH (Spain)	<u>c</u>ircus
ch	CH	<u>ch</u>eese
d, between vowels	TH	bro<u>th</u>er
d, end of word	soft or silent	
g + a, o, u	G	<u>g</u>argle
g + e, i	H	<u>H</u>awaii

h	silent	(Z-z-z-z!)
j	"H" with an	
	attitude; slight "KH"	**h**ot dog
ll	YUH (Mexico)	**y**oyo
	LYUH (Spain)	Wi**lli**am
ñ	NYA	Ta**nya**
qu	K	**c**ookies
r	slight roll or "d"	
	sound	la**dd**er
rr	rolled; the	
	tongue flaps	V**rrr**ooom!
s	SS	**s**paghetti
x between vowels	KS	ta**x**i
x before consonants	SS	**x**ylophone
z	SS	**s**plash

Fast-Track Stress Rules

Stress syllables that have accents, as in "me-NÚ" and "SÁ-bado." If a word does not have an accent,

1. Stress the next-to-last syllable of words that end in a vowel or in the consonants "n" or "s," as in "CA-sa," "ca-MI-sa," "za-PA-to," "to-MA-te," "BAI-lan," and "TA-cos."
2. Stress the last syllable of words that end in any other consonant, as in "ha-BLAR," "ver-DAD," and "ho-TEL."

Here is how you chuckle in Spanish . . .

¡JÁ, JÁ, JÁ!
(HA, HA, HA!)

JOKES MENU
★
EL menú de Los chistes

¡GROAN PROVECHO!
(ENJOY!)
ON YOUR MARACA, GET SET, GO!

ANIMALS

★

Los animales

What is a Spanish **squirrel**'s favorite brand of canned spaghetti?

★ *Chef Boy-**ardilla*** *(Chef Boyardee; una ardilla = squirrel)*

Where in Mexico do the hairy cousins of the llama spend their vacations?

★ *in **Alpaca**-pulco* *(Acapulco; una alpaca = relative of the llama with fleece)*

FUN FACT: The alpaca lives high in the Andes Mountains in Peru, Bolivia, and Chile. It produces twelve pounds of wool, which is used to make blankets, serapes, and ponchos. Alpacas come in twenty-two colors. And before they leave for vacation, they alpaca suitcase.

Why does a Spanish **skunk** drink Coca-Cola?

★ *Because it's **zorrillo** thing.* (It's the real thing = Coca-Cola slogan; un zorrillo = skunk)

FUN FACT: Roberto C. Goizueta, who started as a bottler in Miami, was the first Latino to serve as the CEO for the Coca-Cola Company.

What *Star Trek* movie is about an angry Mexican **rabbit**?

★ The Wrath of **Conejo** (Khan; un conejo = rabbit)

FUN FACT: The Maya saw a rabbit in the moon. According to the "Smiling Rabbit" legend, a sneaky rabbit outsmarted a jaguar twice and howled with laughter. One day when the rabbit was swinging on a vine, the jaguar pulled the vine back and hurled the rabbit to the moon. The "Ja ja ja-guar" got the last laugh. ("Ja" sounds like "ha.")

Which art museum in Madrid has spots all over it?

★ the Leo-**Prado** (El Prado = one of the world's top art museums; un leopardo = leopard)

FUN FACT: During the Spanish Civil War, 500 valuable works from the El Prado were shipped to Geneva, Switzerland, for safekeeping. When World War II began, they were sent by train back to Madrid across France, right under the noses of the Germans.

Why doesn't a Mexican **elk** have many friends?

★ *It's very **ante**-social.* (anti-social; un ante = elk)

For what crime-fighting organization does a Mexican **donkey** work?

★ *the Federal **Burro** of Investigation (Bureau; un burro = donkey)*

> **FUN FACT:** "Un mataburros" is slang for a dictionary in Mexico and South America. "Un burro" is also a slang word for someone whose taco, let's say, is "missing a few ingredients."

The Federal Burro of Investigation.

What sport in which two Costa Rican **monkey**s hit a ball back and forth across a net for hours is rather boring?

★ ***mono** tennis (monotonous; un mono = monkey)*

> **FUN FACT:** The howler monkey, the "mono congo," is one of the loudest animals. Its shriek can be heard two miles away. There are howler monkeys in Costa Rica.

What is the favorite TV channel of a South American **porcupine**?

★ **ESPÍN** *(ESPN; un espín = porcupine)*

What do you call a single Mexican **wolf**?

★ *avai-***lobo** *(available; un lobo = wolf)*

FUN FACT: Los Lobos, a Latin group of the '80s, had the huge hit "La Bamba."

What does a Colombian **pig** use to make coffee?

★ *a **puerco**-lator (percolator; un puerco = pig)*

FUN FACT: Hernando de Soto is called the father of America's pork industry. He brought the first thirteen pigs to Florida in 1539. Later he led a herd of 300 pigs from Florida across the southern United States.

What magazine is read by Dumbo's Mexican female cousins?

★ Elle-efante *(Elle; un elefante = elephant)*

FUN FACT: Elephant figurines bring good luck to Mexican homes. Their trunks must be pointing upward. Trunks pointing downward have lost all their good luck.

What do Argentine magicians say to make a **goat** appear?

★ *"**Cabra** cadabra." (Abra; una cabra = goat)*

Who is the masked king of the South American jungle?

★ *the* **León** *Ranger (Lone; un león = lion)*

> **FUN FACT:** He jumps on his horse and shouts, "Hi ho, Selva!" (Silver; jungle) Castilla-León is the largest region of Spain. León was the capital of Spain in Roman times. "El león no es como lo pintan" means "the lion isn't as fierce as it looks."

What kind of motorcycle does a Peruvian pack animal ride?

★ *a* **Llama**-*ha (Yamaha; una llama = relative of the camel without a hump)*

> **FUN FACT:** The llama is used to transport goods in the Andes Mountains. It's on the coat of arms and flag of Peru. When a llama gets mad, it spits.

What was the name of the final battle between a Spanish **beaver** and the land developers who wanted to bulldoze its dam?

★ **Castor**'s *Last Stand (Custer; un castor = beaver)*

What legendary star of Spanish bullfighting ate bananas for snacks?

★ **Mono**-*lete (Manolete = a great Spanish bullfighter; un mono = monkey)*

> **FUN FACT:** Manolete, called "El Monstruo," was in the bullring at age twelve. He was gored by a bull named Islero when he was thirty and died.

What clay pot is shaped like a small South American rodent and grows green fur when you water it?

★ *a chin-Chia Pet* (una chinchilla = small rodent found in the Andes)

   FUN FACT: The Chia Pet originated in Oaxaca, Mexico, where pottery is a major craft. Three "chias" for its creator.

Why didn't the Mexican sell his car to the lady **giraffe**?

★ *Because **jirafa** was too low.* (her offer; una jirafa = giraffe)

What does a Spanish **zebra** use to cut wood?

★ *a **cebra** saw* (sabre; una cebra = zebra)

What two-ton Venezuelan animal with a horn never knows the answers?

★ *a ri-**no-sé**-ronte* (un rinoceronte = rhinoceros; no sé = I don't know)

What book do Spanish **foxes** consult to look up synonyms?

★ *a thes-**zorros*** (thesaurus; un zorro = fox)

Why does the Mexican **tiger** politician have a good reputation among voters?

★ *It has a lot of in-**tigre**-ty.* (integrity; un tigre = tiger)

What school do South American **spotted cat**s attend
to learn magic?

★ *the **Jaguar**ts School of Witchcraft and Wizardry*
(Hogwarts; un jaguar = jaguar)

FUN FACT: Jaguar gods of the Central and South American
Indians symbolized the power and beauty of nature. An Indian
legend says that the jaguar rubbed mud on itself and that's how
it got its spots.

Who throws the passes when Spanish farm animals
play football?

★ *the quarter-**vaca*** *(quarterback; una vaca = cow)*

The quarter-vaca throws the winning touchdown pass.

What do you call a cross between a Spanish **cow** and
Victor Hugo?

★ *The Hunch-**vaca*** *of Notre Dame (Hunchback; una vaca = cow)*

Where do Mexican **cows** get their morning coffee?

★ *at Star-**vacas*** *(Starbucks; una vaca = cow)*

What fruity round candies with holes in them are popular with South American **zebras**?

★ *Life **Cebras*** *(Life Savers; una cebra = zebra)*

What South American holiday honors working **snakes**?

★ ***Culebra** Day (Labor Day; una culebra = snake)*

FUN FACT: A "teleculebra" is a soap opera in Mexico. Some Mexican soaps are: "El Juego de la Vida" ("The Game of Life"), "Corazón salvaje" ("Wild Heart"), "Amor Real" ("Real Love"), and "Clase 406."

What is in the middle of a Spanish female **boar**'s tummy?

★ ***jabalí** button (her belly button; un jabalí = wild boar)*

What lullaby does an Argentine gaucho sing to his **horse**?

★ *"Rock **caballo** baby" (Rock-a-bye; un caballo = horse)*

FUN FACT: The horse was brought to the Americas by Christopher Columbus in 1493. The gaucho is a cattle herder on the South American plains.

What small Spanish animal has spines and sings about R.E.S.P.E.C.T.?

★ ***Eriza** Franklin (Aretha; una eriza = female hedgehog)*

Which two microscopic Mexican organisms bark?

★ the **perro**-mecium and the **perro**-tozoa *(paramecium; protozoa; un perro = dog)*

> **FUN FACT:** Capitán, Moctezuma, Princesa, Cucaracha, Guido, Dogui, Burrito, Chico, Medor, Tango, Tonto, Ortega, Atila, and Diamante are common names for Spanish dogs.

What small furry pet do girls from Latin America put on their heads?

★ a **gerbo** *(hair bow; un gerbo = gerbil)*

What did the Spanish husband say (with a Boston accent) when his wife asked who was throwing acorns out of the trees?

★ *"Squirrels are, dear."* *(una ardilla = squirrel)*

What do you call a **squid** that hikes in the Spanish Pyrences?

★ a mountain **calamar** *(climber; un calamar = squid)*

> **FUN FACT:** A restaurant called El Calamar Bravo (The Brave Squid) in Zaragoza, Spain, serves squid sandwiches.

What did the skeptical Mexican at the laundromat say when he found out the **spotted cat** had twenty loads of laundry to do?

★ *"That's a lot of **jag-uar**sh."* *(hogwash; un jaguar = jaguar)*

What large water beast at the Spanish zoo is studying to be a wizard?

★ Harry **Hipopótamo** *(Hipo-Potter-mo; un hipopótamo = hippopotamus)*

What NFL team is made up of animals from Peru?

★ the Green Bay **Alpacas** *(Packers; una alpaca = member of the camel family)*

FUN FACT: The Incas domesticated the alpaca. Alpacas communicate to their babies with a clucking sound. They hum and they shriek when frightened.

What Beatles song did the Mexican pop singer **lizard** record?

★ **"Iguana** *Hold Your Hand"* *(I Want to; una iguana = a tropical lizard)*

FUN FACT: In Mexico the iguana is roasted. Its meat is also put in tamales or in stews. Iguana is a Mexican Internet search engine (www.iguana.com.mx).

What Mexican actor played a genetically super-charged reptile in a *Star Trek* film?

★ **Lagarto** *Montalbán (Ricardo; un lagarto = lizard)*

FUN FACT: Ricardo Montalbán, born in Mexico City, played Mr. Roarke on "Fantasy Island" and made over eighty films. He is best known for playing the ruthless Khan in *Star Trek—The Wrath of Khan.*

What Cuban **cat** loved Lucy?

★ *Ricky Ri-**gato*** *(Ricardo; un gato = cat)*

> **FUN FACT:** Mexican cats don't have nine lives. They have seven lives. Cuban Desi Arnaz played the husband and bandleader in the '50s TV classic "I Love Lucy."

Why can't a South American **monkey** learn a foreign language?

★ *Because it's **mono**-lingual. (monolingual; un mono = monkey)*

> **FUN FACT:** "¿Tengo monos en la cara?" ("Do I have monkeys on my face?") means "What are you staring at?"

What Spanish fairy tale is about a blonde girl who sneaks into the house of three **bears** who are professional violinists?

★ Los Tres Virtu-**osos** *(Los Tres Osos = Goldilocks and the Three Bears; un oso = bear)*

> **FUN FACT:** Goldilocks is known as Ricitos Dorados, Ricitos de oro, Bucles de Oro, and Rubita in the Spanish-speaking world.

What big angry beast do Spanish campers never want to meet in the woods?

★ *a furry **oso** that's **oso furioso** (oh so; un oso = bear; furioso = furious)*

> **FUN FACT:** "El oso Teddy" is a Teddy bear. The Care Bears are "los Ositos Cariñositos." "¡Qué oso!" means "How embarrassing!"

Which "Friends" star's Spanish pet was very lazy?

★ *Matthew Perry's* **oso** *(un oso = bear; perezoso = lazy)*

> **FUN FACT:** The bear is the symbol of Madrid. A twenty-ton
> sculpture of a bear called "The Bear and the Madroño Tree"
> stands in the Puerta del Sol square in the center of Madrid.

What is the name of the Leonardo da Vinci painting of
the smiling **female monkey**?

★ **Mona** *Lisa (una mona = female monkey; mona = cute)*

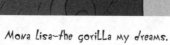
Mona Lisa—the gorilLa my dreams.

What film is about a South American **frog** that keeps
living the same day over and over again?

★ G-**rana** Hog Day *(Groundhog Day; una rana = frog)*

> **FUN FACT:** The ancient Olmecs of Mexico believed the frog
> was the god of rebirth. It ate its own skin and was then reborn.
> It kept coming back as itself over and over again. You could say
> that each time it came back, it was a "re-rana."

What do Colombian **frogs** learn before they travel to swamps in other countries?

★ *fo-**rana** languages (foreign; una rana = frog)*

   FUN FACT: Spanish frogs sound like "Cruá cruá." Argentine frogs go "Berp" and Peruvian frogs sound like "Croac croac."

What was the artistic period of sixteenth-century Mexican swamps?

★ *The **Rana**-ssance (Renaissance; una rana = frog)*

   FUN FACT: The major artist of the Rana-ssance period was Michelangelo Buonarrotti or Buo-**rana**-rotti. At sunset the South American clown tree frog starts croaking and sounds like it's laughing. It has red toes that look like clown shoes, and its body is burgundy with big gold splotches.

What do South Americans call the second-place finisher in a **frog** jumping contest?

★ *the **rana**-up (runner-up; una rana = frog)*

   FUN FACT: The poison dart frog of South America comes in brilliant red, blue, and yellow. Two or three drops of the poison the size of grains of sand can kill an adult human.

What kind of pets do Latin American computer owners have?

★ *los **peces** (PCs; los peces = fish)*

   FUN FACT: Some computer terms in Spanish are "hacer clic," "emailear," "la compu," "chatear," and "surfear." "Cambiar (to change) el chip" in Mexico means to change the way you think about something.

What movie is about a Spanish **frog** that always hops away from the altar before she can say "I do"?

★ **Rana**-way Bride *(Runaway; una rana = frog)*

> **FUN FACT:** "Señor Frog's" is a chain of hoppin' dance clubs in Mexico. One night in 1977 in Culiacan, Mexico, it rained frogs. A tornado had sucked up frogs from a local pond and then dropped them over Culiacan.

There goes the rana-way bride again!

ART

EL arte

What is a revolutionary Mexican artist called?

★ *a Zap-artista (Zapatista = follower of Emiliano Zapata, a Mexican revolutionary hero and reformer)*

FUN FACT: Emiliano Zapata (1879–1919) was a leader in the Mexican Revolution who tried to regain stolen land for the poor farmers of southern Mexico. He died a martyr. People say he still appears on moonlit nights in the hills of Oaxaca on his white horse.

What does an artistic Mexican spotted pony say when it picks up a brush?

★ *"Pinto." (Pinto = I paint)*

FUN FACT: "Pintarlo de color rosa" means "to look at life through rose-colored glasses."

What did Arnold Schwarzenegger do at the famous **art museum** in Madrid?

★ *He took a **Prado** tour. (Predator; El Prado = art museum in Madrid)*

> **FUN FACT:** Because of space limitations, El Prado only has 1,500 paintings of its collection of 9,000 works on display. The museum has works by the Spanish artists Goya, Velázquez, El Greco, and Picasso as well as those of Italian and other international masters.

What Mexican artist's equipment do you get when you cross a ten-gallon hat and Big Foot?

★ *a cowboy Yeti (un caballete = easel)*

What does a Spanish ghost say when it draws?

★ *"Di-boo-jo." (Dibujo = I draw; I am drawing)*

What is a Spanish painting of a dessert with two crusts and fruit called?

★ *a pie-saje (un paisaje = landscape)*

What does a South American watercolor artist put on hot dogs?

★ *acuar-elish (relish; una acuarela = watercolor painting)*

What did the Mexican artist call his paintings of canned pasta?

★ *Spaghetti-Óleos (SpaghettiO's; un óleo = oil painting)*

How did the Latin American artist feel while his paintings were being judged?

★ *He was on **pinceles** and needles.* (pins; un pincel = a paintbrush)

What are the nutritional guidelines for a Mexican artist's palette?

★ *The paints should be high in **colores** and low in **color-esterol**.* (calories; cholesterol; unos colores = colors; un color = color)

What kind of Cuban pasta is **red**?

★ *maca-**rojo**-ni* (macaroni; rojo = red)

FUN FACT: Red is one color of the Mexican and Spanish flags. The bullfighter's cape, called "una muleta," is red.

What did the Venezuelan birdwatcher exclaim when she saw **green** in the sunset?

★ *"Look at the **verde** in the sky."* (birdie; verde = green)

How did the Moroccan man welcome his Spanish friend **Blanca** to his **house**?

★ *"Mi **casa** es su casa, **Blanca**."* (una casa = house; blanca = white [feminine], Blanche; Casablanca = Moroccan seaport)

FUN FACT: "Mi casa es su casa" ("My house is your house") means "Make yourself at home." Spanish speakers call the White House "la Casa Blanca."

What song is a cross between the Blues Brothers and the Spanish version of the **Blue** Man Group?

★ *"I'm **Azul** Man." (Soul; azul = blue)*

FUN FACT: At Agua Azul (Blue Water) in Chiapas, Mexico, there are over 500 waterfalls and pools with turquoise-blue water. The waterfalls range from small 10-foot ones to over 100-foot-high falls. Misol Ma in Chiapas is 125 feet high.

Which Latin American rapper wears **yellow** parachute pants?

★ *MC **Amarillo** (MC Hammer; amarillo = yellow)*

FUN FACT: Amarillo, Texas, is in the Texas Panhandle. The name comes from the yellowish soil along the banks of Amarillo Lake and the fields of yellow flowers.

What Spanish color do you get when you fry bacon?

★ ***gris** (grease; gris = gray)*

What children's song is a cross between the Spanish color **red** and two oars?

★ *"**Rojo**, rojo, rojo your boat." (Row; rojo = red)*

FUN FACT: Mayan pyramids used to be brilliant red with designs in other colors. A red dye called "cochineal," made from parasites from the prickly-pear cactus, is used to color fabrics woven in Mexico and South America.

What do Spanish artists call painting with Coco Puffs or Lucky Charms?

★ *el cerealismo* *(el cereal; el surrealismo = surrealism)*

> **FUN FACT:** The surrealists, such as Miró and Dalí, did not paint the real world, but "mindscapes"—unrealistic scenes with images from dreams and fantasies.

Spanish "cerealist" artists painted at breakfast.

What style of art do you get when you put a Picasso painting in the freezer?

★ *Ice **Cubismo*** *(cubism = modern art style)*

> **FUN FACT:** In cubism, objects are broken up into their basic geometric shapes and then rearranged on a canvas. Pablo Picasso was a pioneer of cubism.

What Spanish color is a cheer for an Olympic sprinter named Anna?

★ **"Anaranjada"** *(Anna, run harder; anaranjada = orange, feminine form)*

Who was the most famous lizard painter of Spain?

★ *El Gecko (gecko; El Greco = artist of the Mannerism style)*

FUN FACT: Domenicos Theotokopoulos (1541–1614) simply wrote "El Greco" ("the Greek") on his paintings. Because he distorted the human figure, his critics thought he needed glasses or was going mad. He was dabbling in abstract art before it existed.

What does a Mexican mural painter read in the newspaper every morning?

★ *his **Orozco**pe (horoscope; José Orozco = Mexican muralist painter)*

FUN FACT: José Orozco (1883–1949) painted the misery and suffering of the Mexican people in murals. He had only one hand because of an accidental childhood gunpowder explosion. Orozco painted murals at Dartmouth College in New Hampshire.

What do Spanish art experts call melting clocks etched in your mind?

★ *an in-**dalí**-ble image (indelible; Salvador Dalí = surrealist painter)*

FUN FACT: Salvador Dalí (1904–1989) was an eccentric artist with a wide handlebar moustache. *The Persistence of Memory* has melting clocks in it that were inspired by a Camembert cheese he was eating one day.

Which doll with red yarn hair was named after a modern architect from Barcelona?

★ *Rag-***gaudí** *Ann (Raggedy; Antoni Gaudí = modern Spanish architect)*

FUN FACT: Antoni Gaudí (1852–1926) designed cool, avant-garde colorful parks, furniture, and distorted buildings that seemed to move. When hit by a trolley, people thought he was a poor beggar. No one would drive him to the hospital. He died three days later in a hospital for poor people.

What did the wicked queen from *Snow White* say as she looked at the surrealist painting in the Spanish museum?

★ *"***Miró**, *Miró, on the wall." (mirror; Joan Miró = Spanish surrealist painter)*

FUN FACT: Joan Miró (1893–1983) painted abstract paintings with warped objects, twisted shapes, and squiggly lines. He did murals for a Cincinnati hotel and for Harvard University.

What did the Spanish art dealer tell the customer who thought the portrait of Charles IV was a copy?

★ *"I assure you it's the real Mc***Goya**." *(McCoy; Francisco Goya = Spanish artist)*

FUN FACT: Francisco Goya (1746–1828) was the royal court painter for Charles IV. He secretly mocked the royal family in an unattractive portrait. The horrors of war and his loss of hearing made him bitter and brutally honest.

What kind of tennis shoes did the great seventeenth-century Spanish artist of the Golden Age wear?

★ *Veláz-Keds (Diego Velázquez = called Spain's greatest painter)*

> **FUN FACT:** Diego Velázquez (1599–1660) was the Baroque portrait painter of Phillip IV and the curator of the king's art collection. In 1660 he planned the wedding of the king's daughter, the Infanta María Teresa, to Louis XIV of France.

Which famous Spanish artist oinks while he paints?

★ *Pablo Pigcasso (Picasso = Cubist artist from Spain)*

> **FUN FACT:** Pablo Picasso (1881–1973) had his first exhibit at age thirteen and was a trained artist at age fifteen. His career spanned seventy years. According to *Guinness World Records*, Picasso did 13,500 paintings and over 100,000 other works.

Where did Spanish surrealist artists get their cold cuts and cheeses?

★ *at the Salvador Deli (delicatessen; Salvador Dalí = Spanish surrealist painter)*

> **FUN FACT:** Dalí was afraid of grasshoppers. He did wild publicity stunts. Once when he gave a speech in a diving suit, the metal helmet got stuck and he almost suffocated. The Salvador Dalí Museum in Figueras, Spain, where he is buried, has egg sculptures along its roof.

What Spanish cubist artist was a **failure**?

★ *Pablo* **Fracaso** *(Picasso = Spanish painter; un fracaso = failure)*

> **FUN FACT:** The Pablo Picasso painting called *Boy with a Pipe* sold for $93 million at Sotheby's in New York in 2004. That broke the record for a painting.

What do Mexicans call the cryptic writing on ancient vases?

★ **jarra**-*glyphics* *(hieroglyphics; una jarra = jar)*

> **FUN FACT:** The Maya, according to historians, had the most advanced ancient writing system. It had 800 glyphs that represented whole words or sounds.

BIRDS

Los pájaros

What does a Costa Rican **bird** wear in case its wings stop working?

★ a **pájaro**-chute *(parachute; un párajo = bird)*

FUN FACT: There are 1,380 species of birds in Venezuela.

What do the Latin American people call the science of **bird** flight?

★ **ave**-ation *(aviation; un ave = bird)*

FUN FACT: The Spanish version of Big Bird is a female named Caponata. She has red, yellow, and orange feathers, long eyelashes, and striped legs. The Mexican version of Big Bird is a male named Paco.

Where do large Peruvian birds of prey live?

★ *in **cóndor**-miniums* *(el cóndor)*

> **FUN FACT:** The condor lives high in the Andes of Peru. It is
> 52″ tall, 100″ long, and has a wingspan of up to twelve feet. The
> condor travels up to 200 miles a day. With only one flap of its
> wings, it can soar for an hour.

What do Latin American **ducks** study in medical
school?

★ ***pato**-logy* *(pathology; un pato = duck)*

> **FUN FACT:** "Pato" is an Argentine game on horseback like
> polo. The sound of a duck in Spain is "cruá-cruá." "Al agua, pato"
> means "Let's get going. Let's get to work."

Where in the United States do Venezuelan **parrot**s go
on vacation?

★ *to F-**loro**-da* *(Florida; un loro = parrot)*

> **FUN FACT:** About half of the 340 species of parrots live in
> Central America and South America. The "loro hablador" talks.
> "Un loro" is a radio-cassette player in Spain.

How did the Aztecs greet each other?

★ *"¿Qué tzal?"* *(quetzal = a bright-green iridescent bird of Central
America)*

> **FUN FACT:** The major Aztec god, Quetzalcoatl, was part
> quetzal. The male's tail is twenty-four inches to four feet long. It
> has a red belly and a pink tuft on its head.

Who do Venezuelan birds call when their drains are clogged?

★ *the **paloma*** *(plumber; una paloma = dove)*

FUN FACT: Speaking of plumbing, the ingenious Incas engineered and constructed remarkable water systems over 500 years ago. Some of them are still used today.

Pedro the paLoma at your service!

Which pop singer's career is really soaring?

★ *Christina **Águila**-lera (Aguilera; un águila = eagle)*

FUN FACT: "¿Águila o sol?" in Mexico means "Heads or tails?" Christina María Aguilera's father is from Ecuador. She appeared on "Star Search" at age eight and was a Mickey Mouse Club Mouseketeer before becoming a pop diva at eighteen.

What kind of Mexican TV show has two teams of
peacocks competing on a deserted island?

★ *a **pavo real**-ity show* (reality show; un pavo real = peacock)

What do Colombians call it when a surgeon moves a
hen from one henhouse to another one?

★ *an or-**gallina** transplant* (organ; una gallina = hen)

> **FUN FACT:** "¿La gallina o los huevos?" means "Which came
> first, the chicken or the egg?" "Un (Una) gallina" is a coward.

What Spanish bird played the original James Bond?

★ *Sean **Canario*** (Connery; un canario = canary)

> **FUN FACT:** The Canary Islands, which are a part of Spain, were
> not named after a canary. The Latin name, *Canariae Insulae*,
> means "Island of Dogs."

What well-known, long-legged Mexican bird painted
sunflowers and blazing stars?

★ *Vincent Van **Flamenco*** (Van Gogh; un flamenco = flamingo)

> **FUN FACT:** The Río Lagartos ("Lizard River") on the northern
> coast of the Yucatán Peninsula in Mexico is a bird refuge. It has
> 30,000 pink flamingos.

Which Mexican barnyard ballet dancer was heavy on
its feet?

★ ***Pavo**-lova* (Pavlova; un pavo = turkey)

What do Puerto Rican **rooster**s do for relaxation and meditation?

★ **Gallo**-*ga* *(Yoga; un gallo = rooster)*

FUN FACT: "¡Qué gallo!" means "What a handsome guy!"

The Puerto Rican rooster does Gallo-ga to relax.

What did the South American **chicken** say to his stressed-out pal who was losing it?

★ **"Pollo** yourself together." *(Pull yourself; un pollo = chicken)*

FUN FACT: El Pollo Loco (The Crazy Chicken) is a fried chicken restaurant chain in Latin America. The chain is now in Arizona, New Mexico, and California.

Where do Bolivian **lark**s wash their clothes?

★ at **alondra**-*mat* *(laundromat; una alondra = lark)*

What do Mexicans say to make **geese** appear?

★ **"Ocas** pocus." *(hocus-pocus; una oca = goose)*

What do two ostriches from a Spanish zoo do to end an argument?

★ *They call an aves-truce.* *(truce; un avestruz = ostrich)*

FUN FACT: The famous "Voladores de Papantla" spin around high poles, four men at a time, hanging by their ankles on ropes, and dressed in bird costumes.

What bird at the Mexican zoo gets spares and strikes?

★ *a bowling **pingüino*** *(bowling pin; un pingüino = penguin)*

FUN FACT: "Pingüinos" are chocolate cream-filled cupcakes in Mexico.

What video game character is a female Venezuelan bird that raids tombs?

★ **Lora** *Croft (Lara; una lora = female parrot)*

FUN FACT: Venezuela has forty-eight species of parrots. The colorful birds fly free in the jungles.

What do Mexican turkeys order at their local Starbucks?

★ **guaja**-*lattes (lattes; un guajalote = wild turkey)*

FUN FACT: The word "guajalote" is slang in Mexico for a fool.

What is a Latin American **woodpecker**'s favorite soda?

★ **Cuco**-cola. *(Coca-Cola; un cuco = woodpecker)*

What is the sound of a wise Spanish bird crying?

★ **Búho** *(boo hoo; un búho = owl)*

What did the Aztecs call a rainbow of chewy candies in the shape of birds?

★ *Sk-etzals (Skittles; un quetzal = tropical bird of Mexico and Central America)*

FUN FACT: Quetzal dances are performed in Mexico with huge colorful headdresses that are five feet wide.

How do South American birds order in a restaurant?

★ **ala** carte *(à la carte; un ala = wing)*

What did the Colombian salesman at the home improvement store tell the **hummingbird** who was looking at samples of flooring?

★ *"**Picaflor**. Any floor." (Pick a floor; un picaflor = hummingbird)*

FUN FACT: Mexico has fifty varieties of hummingbirds.

CALENDAR AND CELEBRATIONS

★

EL calendario y Las fiestas

What trendy store at Mexican malls puts **dates** on T-shirts?

★ *Abercrombie and **Fecha*** *(Abercrombie and Fitch; la fecha = date)*

FUN FACT: The Mayan solar calendar had 365.25 days.

Why are koala bears in Mexican zoos always born in the spring?

★ *Because they are **marzo**-pials. (marsupial; marzo = March)*

> **FUN FACT:** "Las Fallas" is Valencia's outrageous festival of fire. Nearly 350 multi-story satirical papier-mâché sculptures, taking months to construct, are displayed in parks. At midnight on March 19, they are torched. The city is all flames and firecrackers.

What can you say about the Latin American woman who barely avoided a car accident on New Year's Day?

★ *She had **enero** escape. (a narrow; enero = January)*

> **FUN FACT:** January 17 is the Fiesta de San Antonio Abad, the patron saint of animals, amputees, brush makers, and skin diseases. Pets and farm animals in Mexico are dressed up in ribbons, bangles, and bows and paraded to church for blessings.

What do you call a Mexican who can see beyond April?

★ ***mayo**-pic (myopic; mayo = May)*

What brand of potato chips is eaten in South America in the middle of the week?

★ *Miérco-Lays (Lays; miércoles = Wednesday)*

What are the basic groceries Mexicans buy to get through **Friday**?

★ *the **viernes**-cessities (bare necessities; viernes = Friday)*

What cereal do Latin Americans eat in early summer?

★ ***Junio*** *Bunches of Oats (Honey; junio = June)*

What sport is played on **Thursdays** in Cuba?

★ ***jueves***-*ball (baseball; jueves = Thursday)*

FUN FACT: Thursday the 13th and Tuesday the 13th are both bad luck days in Latin America.

What kind of Latin American physician operates at the beginning of the year?

★ ***enero*** *surgeon (a neurosurgeon; enero = January)*

FUN FACT: In San Sebastián, Spain, for twenty-four hours from midnight January 19 to January 20, parades of drummers march around the city, pounding on their drums. It's called "La Tamborrada."

Why did it take the Spanish man an extra **month** to build his house?

★ *He **mes**-calculated. (miscalculated; el mes = month)*

What would you call a law that made Spanish people commute to work on pogo sticks on **Monday**s?

★ *sheer **lunes**-cy (lunacy; lunes = Monday)*

FUN FACT: The first day of the week on a Spanish calendar is Monday.

What technology involving plastic strands and dots of light is popular among Mexicans who buy lamps in the winter?

★ **febrero** optics *(fiber optics; febrero = February)*

FUN FACT: The expression "el día 30 de febrero" (February 30) means "never."

How do Latin Americans send letters to people **yesterday**?

★ **ayer**-*mail* *(airmail; ayer = yesterday)*

FUN FACT: "No nací ayer" means "I wasn't born yesterday."

What do Spanish people use in the spring to scour their frying pans?

★ **abril**-*o pad* *(Brillo pad; abril = April)*

What French emperor's Spanish cousin puts off things until **tomorrow**?

★ *Charle***mañana** *(Charlemagne; mañana = tomorrow)*

FUN FACT: "Mañana" in Mexico may also mean "in the near future." People there have a less pressured, laid-back attitude about deadlines.

What Spanish artist was known for painting on **Saturday**?

★ **Sábado** *Dalí (Salvador Dalí; sábado = Saturday)*

What does a Spanish sailor reply when his commander gives him orders to carry out **today**?

★ *"**Hoy**, hoy, señor."* *(Ay, ay; hoy = today)*

What actor who played Zorro is reaching the **fall** of his life?

★ **Otoño** *Banderas (Antonio; el otoño = fall, autumn)*

> **FUN FACT:** Antonio Banderas played soccer until he was injured and then became an actor. He starred in *The Mambo Kings*, *The Mask of Zorro*, and *Spy Kids*. He is the voice of Puss-in-Boots in *Shrek 2*.

What store do Mexican shoppers go to on **Tuesdays**?

★ *Wal-**martes*** *(Walmart; martes = Tuesday)*

What Spanish month is known for having the most current events?

★ *DC-iembre (DC [electricity]; diciembre = December)*

> **FUN FACT:** December 28 is "el Día de los Inocentes" in Spanish-speaking countries. In some Latin American countries it is also April Fool's Day.

What little indentations are on Pablo's face just for **today**?

★ *Dimples, because they are **hoy**-üelos. (los hoyuelos = dimples; hoy = today)*

What game about following orders do Spanish children play on a **week**ly basis?

★ **Semana** *Says* (Simon; una semana = week)

What is a detective who tracks down a **party** in a Nicaraguan swamp?

★ *an in-**fiesta**-gator* (investigator; una fiesta = party)

FUN FACT: There are around 5,000 cultural and religious festivals in Mexico each year.

Who was the **party** animal of the Mexican version of *The Addams Family*?

★ *Uncle **Fiesta**, of course* (Fester; una fiesta = party)

FUN FACT: In Mexico "Vamos de reventón" means "Let's party."

How did Luke Skywalker and his *Star Wars* friends celebrate the Jedi master's birthday?

★ *with a Pin-Yoda* (piñata = decorated container with candy and toys)

FUN FACT: Piñatas were originally decorated clay pots filled with candy. The Aztecs and the Maya filled them with treasures, put them on a pole, and smashed them with a stick. The goodies inside that fell out were intended to please the gods.

What do you say when you cross a Mexican birthday with the Nutty Professor?

★ *"Feliz Klump-eaños"* (Feliz cumpleaños = Happy Birthday)

What do people in Latin America shout as they count down to the new year?

★ *"**Año** mark, get set, go!"* (un año = year; Día del Año Nuevo = New Year's Day)

FUN FACT: On New Year's Eve, Spanish people swallow one grape with each toll of the midnight bells for good luck for the next year. In Ecuador, life-sized puppets that mock politicians are made for "Años Viejos." At midnight, the puppets are burned along with any bad memories of the past year for a fresh start.

What Mexican holiday celebrates the extremities of women's feet?

★ *El Día de los **Mujer**-toes* (El Día de los Muertos = The Day of the Dead; una mujer = woman, wife)

FUN FACT: Mexicans celebrate the return of the spirits of loved ones from October 31 to November 2. Families decorate graves with flowers, candles, and the favorite foods of the deceased. Children eat sugar and chocolate skulls, hearses, and skeletons.

What boys' band is named after a Mexican holiday?

★ *'N **Cinco de Mayo*** ('N SYNC; el Cinco de Mayo = Mexican national holiday)

FUN FACT: The Cinco de Mayo is a holiday of unity and patriotism. It celebrates Mexico's victory in 1862 at the Battle of Puebla by General Zaragoza over a bigger French army. It wasn't until 1867, though, that the Emperor Maximilian finally left.

How did Seinfeld's friend Elaine describe the Mexican birthday party?

★ **"Piñata**, *yadda, yadda"* (una piñata)

FUN FACT: Today piñatas are made of papier mâché and come in creative shapes such as animals, cartoon characters, dinosaurs, monster trucks, fish, parrots, lips, hearts, or chickens. A giant piñata appeared in 1990 at the Carnival Miami, weighing ten thousand pounds and standing 27 feet tall.

What holiday celebrates all Spanish-speaking heritages and makes past mistakes disappear?

★ *El Día del Eraser* (El Día de la Raza = the Day of the Race)

FUN FACT: El Día de la Raza (de la Hispanidad) is celebrated on October 12, Columbus Day. It celebrates the heritages and cultures that make up Latin America.

On what day do Hispanic people celebrate odors?

★ *El Día del Scento* (El Día del Santo = saint's day)

FUN FACT: Spanish-speaking people celebrate the saint's days of the saints after which they are named. So they get to celebrate not one but two "birthdays" every year!

What do tiny Mexican insects say to congratulate each other?

★ *"Fleas-cidades."* (felicidades = congratulations)

What does a Japanese girl living in Mexico say to her childhood when she turns fifteen?

★ *"Quin-Sayonara."* *(una quinceañera = fifteenth birthday of Hispanic girls; quince = fifteen; años = years)*

FUN FACT: Mexican girls enter womanhood with a wedding-like celebration that includes a mariachi serenade, beautiful gown, mass, court of seven couples, and big party. The girl's last doll is on display, and her father puts her first pair of high heels on her. There are quinceañera Barbie dolls.

What Latin American holiday is dedicated to a dull employed clove of **garlic**?

★ *El Día del Drab **Ajo*** *(Trabajo = Labor Day; un ajo = clove of garlic)*

FUN FACT: El Día del Trabajo is on May 1st in Mexico and many other Spanish-speaking countries.

What Mexican store sells red and green fleece shirts at **Christmas** time?

★ *Old **Navidad*** *(Old Navy; Navidad = Christmas)*

What service do Latin Americans use for their cars when they go to the Mardi Gras parade?

★ *They use Carna-valet parking.* *(Carnaval = Carnival festival before Lent)*

CRAZY

★

¡Muy Loco!

What store at a Spanish mall sells crazy athletic shoes?

★ *Foot **Loca*** *(Foot Locker; loca [loco] = crazy)*

FUN FACT: San Miguel de Allende, Mexico, has an annual Loco Day. In *Los Locos Addams* (*The Addams Family*), Thing is Dedos (fingers) and Lurch is Largo. He says, "¿Llamó usted, Señor?" ("You rang, Sir?")

What Ricky Martin hit song is about a crazy nacho cheese spread?

★ *"Livin' the Velveeta **Loca**"* *("Livin' the Vida Loca" = Livin' the Crazy Life)*

FUN FACT: Ricky Martin, from Puerto Rico, sang in the teen group Menudo. He was in a Mexican soap opera, the play *Les Misérables* on Broadway, and the soap opera "General Hospital." He was the voice of Disney's Hercules and won a Grammy in 1999.

Why can't the man from Chile see the **tail** of an animal?

★ *He's **cola** blind.* *(color; una cola = tail)*

What Latin American store sells **ugly** toys?

★ ***Feo** Schwarz (F.A.O.; feo = ugly)*

What candy gives Mexican people a lot of **laughs**?

★ ***Risas** Peanut Butter Cups (Reese's; una risa = laugh)*

FUN FACT: "La risa es el mejor remedio" means "Laughter is the best medicine."

When do Spanish people **eat** snacks while they're watching TV?

★ *during the **comer**-cials (comer = to eat)*

FUN FACT: "Las botanas" are snacks. In Spain, Matutano makes Cheetos Futebolas cheese puffs in the shape of soccer balls and Cheetos Pandilla/Fantasmas, which are potato crisps in the shape of bats and ghosts. In Mexico, people snack on Barcel's Catsup Papas, chips with ketchup packets included, and Maizitos that are chile-and-lime-flavored chips.

What is the favorite dessert of Spanish e-mailers?

★ *mince-aje pie (un mensaje = message)*

What did the worn-out Spanish dancer say?

★ *"I can **baile** move." (barely; un baile = dance; bailar = to dance)*

What is the name of the Spanish **bread maker** who never grows old?

★ *Peter **Panadero*** *(Peter Pan; un panadero = baker)*

> **FUN FACT:** In the Spanish version of *Peter Pan*, Tinkerbell is "Campanilla," Captain Hook is "el Capitán Garfio," and Neverland is "el País de Nunca Jamás."

What '50s Mexican song is about a lilac **paper** shredder?

★ *"Purple **Papel** Eater"* *(People; el papel = paper)*

What do you get when you cross John Steinbeck and Spanish **staples**?

★ *"The **Grapas** of Wrath"* *(Grapes; una grapa = staple)*

What Latin American fairy tale character covered everything with **tape**?

★ ***Cinta**-rella* *(Cinderella; la cinta = adhesive tape)*

> **FUN FACT:** "Cinderella" is "Cenicienta" in Spanish.

What do they show on the Spanish news after a handball game?

★ *the jai a-lights* *(highlights; el jai alai [la pelota] = handball)*

> **FUN FACT:** The ball in jai alai can move at up to 180 miles per hour.

What do people of South America call a man of **iron** who saves the day?

★ *a super **hierro*** *(hero; el hierro = iron)*

What do Spanish people take to calm their nerves when they travel by rail?

★ ***tren**-quilizers* *(tranquilizers; un tren = train)*

FUN FACT: The Chihuahua-Pacific line in northern Mexico is a seventeen-hour 400-mile trip through the steep Sierra Madre mountains and canyons. The views are breathtaking as the train snakes through the mountains up to 8,000 feet above sea level.

What happened to the Mexican card player who departed mysteriously, leaving a card with the **three** of hearts on the table?

★ *He disappeared without a **tres**.* *(trace; tres = three)*

What did the first little Puerto Rican pig say when the wolf threatened to blow down his **straw** house?

★ *"Pura **paja**."* *(pura paja = nonsense, literally "pure straw")*

What do you get when you cross the NBA with Mexican **hairsprays**?

★ *the Los Angeles **Lacas*** *(Lakers; la laca = hair spray)*

Waiting in line at a pump at a Mexican service station is like what vegetable to José?

★ *asparagus* *(espera gas; espera = he waits for)*

What do you call a Spanish man who imagines he has the **hiccups**?

★ an **hipo**-*chondriac* (hypochondriac; un hipo = hiccup)

What does a Spanish procrastinator put on his hot dog?

★ **más-tarde** (mustard; más tarde = later)

What did the woman call the Mexican **jeweler** who saved her life?

★ "My **joyero**." (hero; un joyero = jeweler)

What is the mood of Latin American shoppers who attack clearance racks?

★ They are **ganga** ho. (gung ho; una ganga = bargain)

What are Cubans doing when they stomp on Macintoshes?

★ the apple **salsa** (sauce; la salsa = Latin dance with African influences)

What does Seinfeld's neighbor put on when he lies on a beach in Cancún?

★ Kremer **bronceadora** (la crema bronceadora = suntan cream)

What do Latin American people call **ugly** pictures?

★ fotogra**feas** (una fotografía = photograph; feas = ugly [feminine plural])

Who gave Spanish people the idea to take a two-hour afternoon **nap**?

★ *their an-**siesta**s (ancestors; una siesta = afternoon nap or break)*

What do Mexicans take when bad **jokes** give them indigestion?

★ **Broma**-*Seltzer (Bromo-Seltzer; una broma = joke)*

   FUN FACT: Paul Rodríguez and George López, who has his own TV show, are very successful Mexican-American comedians.

What does the **Pope** eat for breakfast when he's in South America?

★ **Papa** *Tarts (Pop Tarts; el Papa = pope)*

What do Spanish mothers put on babies when they diaper them to make them strong?

★ *baby **poder** (powder; el poder = strength, power)*

   FUN FACT: "Querer es poder" ("to want is to be able") means "Where there's a will, there's a way."

What color is **ice** in Spain?

★ *Yellow, because it's **hielo**. (el hielo = ice)*

What did the Mexican Ken doll say when be broke up with his famous girlfriend?

★ **"Hasta la vista**, *Barbie." (Baby; hasta la vista = So long, see you later)*

What do you get when you cross Ernest Hemingway with a Mexican fast-food chain?

★ For Whom the Taco Bell Tolls *(For Whom the Bell Tolls = Hemingway's novel about the Spanish Civil War)*

FUN FACT: In *The Sun Also Rises*, Ernest Hemingway wrote about Pamplona, Spain, and bullfighting. There is a bronze statue of Hemingway outside the Plaza de Toros in Pamplona.

Which actor from the Mexican version of "That '70s Show" is a good **listen**er?

★ Ashton **Escucha** *(Kutcher; escucha = he/she listens, is listening)*

What Latin American superhero climbs up the sides of buildings and is a fencing expert?

★ **Espada**-*Man (Spider Man, una espada = sword)*

FUN FACT: "Spider-Man" is "El hombre araña" in Spanish.

What Spanish TV crime show is about a cheddar left in the refrigerator for many years?

★ "Cold **Queso**" *(Case; un queso = cheese)*

What does Casper say when he meets spirits in Spanish haunted houses?

★ "**Mucho** ghost-o" *(Mucho gusto = Nice to meet you)*

What language do Spanish babies speak?

★ es-**pañal** *(español = Spanish; un pañal = diaper)*

What language do Mexicans speak when they're skiing in Colorado?

★ *Aspen-ñol (español = Spanish)*

> **FUN FACT:** Spanish is spoken by 400 million people and is tied with English for the second most spoken world language. In Spain the majority speaks Castilian Spanish, a dialect where a *z* or *c* (with *e* or *i*) sounds like "th."

Where do Mexicans with **coughs** go?

★ *to **Tos** "R" Us ("Toys "R" Us; uná tos = cough)*

> **FUN FACT:** "No hay tos" is a Mexican expression that means "No problem."

Why does the student at the Puerto Rican auto school make only right turns when he drives?

★ *Because **izquierda** turn left. (he's scared to; izquierda = left)*

What Chicago institution of higher learning teaches surfing to Mexican students?

★ *La **Ola** University (Loyola; una ola = wave)*

What happened to the Spanish sailor who always answered "**Yes**"?

★ *He got **sí** sick. (sea; sí = yes)*

> **FUN FACT:** In Latin America, nodding doesn't mean agreement. It merely acknowledges what is said. "Simón" is Mexican slang for "Yes" and "Nel" is "no."

What do Mexican **baskets** that are best friends call themselves?

★ *soul cestas* (sisters; una cesta = basket)

How often do Spanish children use their **ruler**s in school?

★ *on a regla basis* (regular; una regla = ruler)

What do Latin Americans call it when an older **man** forgets something?

★ *a señor moment* (senior; un señor = man, gentleman)

What happened to the Argentine dancers when the band played too fast?

★ *They got all tangoed up.* (tangled; el tango = romantic Argentine dance)

FUN FACT: The tango has gliding steps mixed with quick movements and dramatic poses. Heartthrob actor Rudolph Valentino introduced the tango to the world in a film in 1921.

What famous Spanish psychic could predict who would win a **checkers** game?

★ *Nostra-damas* (Nostradamus; las damas = checkers)

What plastic ring do Spanish zoo animals spin around their waists for exercise when they're in their cages?

★ *a jaula hoop* (hula hoop; una jaula = cage)

What do Puerto Ricans call the tiny black-and-white frog that lives on their island?

★ *an Oreo* **coquí** *(cookie; un coquí = tiny Puerto Rican tree frog)*

FUN FACT: The "coquí" is the unofficial symbol of Puerto Rico. It changes color with its surroundings and makes the sound "ko kee ko kee ko kee."

FAMILY

La famiLia

What did the Spanish boy say when he saw his parents, brothers, and sisters in a photo?

★ *"These people look very **familia**."* *(familiar; una familia — family)*

What kind of basketball shoes do Mexican **brothers** wear?

★ **Hermano** *Jordans (Air Jordans; un hermano = brother)*

What is a married Spanish cow?

★ *a moo-jer (una mujer = wife, woman)*

Who did the Spanish female clown bring to the party?

★ *her es-Bozo (un esposo = husband)*

What do you get when you cross Shakespeare with a Latin American **grandmother** who saves the day?

★ All's **Abuela** That Ends Abuela *(All's Well That Ends Well; una abuela = grandmother)*

FUN FACT: In many Latin American homes, three generations live together. Grandmothers chaperone their grandchildren on their dates.

Did the Venezuelan woman know she had a new **daughter-in-law**?

★ *No, she wasn't **nuera** of it. (aware; una nuera = daughter-in-law)*

Which Cuban relative does pirouettes in a tutu?

★ *a **prima** ballerina (una prima = female cousin)*

Which South American relative is in the cast of "Law and Order SVU"?

★ *Ice **Tío** (Ice-T; un tío = uncle)*

FUN FACT: "¡Qué tío!" means "What a great guy!"

What did Señor MacDonald sing when his wife had a baby **daughter**?

★ *"**Hija**, hija, o" (E I E I O; una hija = daughter)*

What do Spanish people call **twins** born in a swamp?

★ *marsh-**gemelos** (marshmallows; unos gemelos = male twins)*

Where in Canada do single Latin American men find **girlfriend**s?

★ in **Novia** Scotia *(Nova; una novia = girlfriend)*

Did you hear about the Mexican trapeze artist who was performing without his **grandson**?

★ *He was working without a **nieto**.* *(net; un nieto = grandson)*

What is a Mexican grandfather's affection for his grandchildren called?

★ **Papi** love *(puppy; Papi = Grandpa)*

What does a Spanish mother tell her little boy when his older **sisters** are going to baby-sit him?

★ *"Mind your **hermanas**."* *(manners; una hermana = sister)*

What kind of refrigerator does a Latin American sister have?

★ an **Hermana** *(Amana; una hermana = sister)*

What does a busy Mexican **godmother** run on?

★ **madrina**-line *(adrenaline; una madrina = godmother)*

What Spanish cereal makes **sons** happy?

★ Cheeri-**hijos** *(Cheerios; unos hijos = children)*

What does a Spanish **wife** put on when she's chilly?

★ a **mujer** sweater *(mohair; una mujer = wife, woman)*

What pocket-sized gadget holds the downloaded songs of a Spanish **father**?

★ an i**Padre** *(iPod; un padre = father)*

FUN FACT: In Mexico "padre" means "marvelous." A "papasote" is a "big daddy." "Padrísimo" means the "very best."

What illness do tired Mexican **brother**s get?

★ **hermano**nucleosis *(mononucleosis; un hermano = brother)*

What energetic relative is like a Spanish amusement park ride?

★ a **tío** vivo *(un tío vivo = lively uncle; un tiovivo = merry-go-round)*

Which Spanish family member is in the alphabet?

★ The brother, because H, I, J, K, el **hermano**, P. *(un hermano = brother)*

What does a Spanish great-grandfather make for lunch?

★ a **bisabuel-o**gna sandwich *(bologna; un bisabuelo = great-grandfather)*

What Mexican relative wears many heavy gold chains?

★ *Mr. **Tío*** *(Mr. T; un tío = uncle)*

What is the favorite beverage of a South American **twin**?

★ ***Gemelo*** *Yellow (Mellow; un gemelo = a male twin)*

FUN FACT: "Los gemelos" are twins. Triplets are "los trillizos."

What do Spanish **relative**s always put around their written sentences?

★ ***pariente**-ses (parentheses; un pariente = relative)*

FASHION

★

La moda

Who dictates **fashion** in a Latin American family?

★ the **moda** (mother; la moda = fashion, style)

FUN FACT: Christy Turlington, a model for Calvin Klein and Maybelline, was the first Hispanic model to earn one million dollars in a year. Her mother is Salvadoran. Elsa Benítez from Sonora, Mexico, is another successful Latin American model.

If you travel from Spain to Romania and run out of things to wear, where are you?

★ at the end of Eu-**ropa** (your rope; la ropa = clothing; Europa = Europe)

FUN FACT: A beach in Zihuatanejo, Mexico, is called the Playa la Ropa (Beach of Clothing). When a Spanish galleon was shipwrecked off its coast, all the clothes on board washed up on the beach.

What Spanish circus performer wears **clothes** that are very snug?

★ *a tight* **ropa** *walker (rope; la ropa = clothing)*

FUN FACT: "La ropa sucia se lava en casa" ("dirty laundry is washed at home") means that family matters should be kept private. "Ropa vieja" ("old clothes") is a soup from Cuba that uses leftover meat.

What do the people in Whoville, Spain, wash every week?

★ *their* **ropa** *Seuss-ia (la ropa sucia = dirty laundry; Dr. Seuss)*

Did you hear about the Spanish **dress**maker who made bad coffee?

★ *She made the* **vestido**. *(best tea, though; un vestido = dress)*

FUN FACT: The fashions of designer Carolina Herrera, a Venezuelan, were worn by Jackie Kennedy Onassis. Herrera also designed Caroline Kennedy's wedding dress.

What does a Mexican kicker for the NFL put on before each game?

★ *his punt-alones (unos pantalones = pants)*

FUN FACT: Jim Plunkett, a Mexican American, was the first Hispanic professional quarterback. As Rookie of the Year with the Boston Patriots in 1971, he threw for 2,158 yards and 19 touchdowns. He worked as a teen to help his parents, who were both blind.

What is a Mexican **hat** vendor's favorite song from *The Wizard of Oz*?

★ *"**Sombrero**-ver the Rainbow"* *(Somewhere; un sombrero = Mexican hat)*

> **FUN FACT:** The wide-brimmed sombrero from Mexico comes from the word "sombra" or shade. It's the ancestor of the cowboy hat. Sombreros are made of straw or felt.

The Mexican hat vendor sings his favorite song from The Wizard of Oz.

What song about having a wonderful day does a Mexican **shoe** vendor sing?

★ *"**Zapato** dee doo dah"* *("Zip-a-dee-doo-dah"; un zapato = shoe)*

> **FUN FACT:** "Zapatero, a tus zapatos" (shoemaker, stick to your shoes) means "mind your own business."

Where in the West Indies do Spanish people run around in their flannel nightwear?

★ in the **Pijamas** *(Bahamas; unos pijamas = pajamas)*

What restaurant chain in Spain sells hamburgers and underwear, too?

★ **Braga** King *(Burger King; una braga = pair of underpants)*

What do Latin Americans call people who can see a **girdle** way in the distance?

★ **faja**-sighted *(far; una faja = a girdle)*

FUN FACT: Little girdles are "fajitas."

Why do **glove**s spread so quickly across Spain?

★ *They are highly **guante**-gious. (contagious; un guante = glove)*

What all-time great Yankees catcher wears **tropical shirts** from Latin America?

★ *Yo-**Guayabera** (Yogi Berra; una guayabera = loose-fitting tropical shirt)*

FUN FACT: The guayabera is two hundred years old. It's called the bowling shirt, Cuban shirt, wedding shirt, or the cigar shirt. It has four pockets and two strips of very narrow pleats.

What famous comedy trio sells **backpack**s in Spain?

★ *Curly, Larry, and* **Mochila** *(Moe; una mochila = backpack)*

What did the record-breaking Mexican **cotton** grower boast?

★ **"Algodón** *in history." (I'll go down; el algodón = cotton)*

FUN FACT: In 1879, Estevan Ochoa was the first pioneer to plant cotton for commercial purposes in Arizona. "El algodón de azúcar" is cotton candy.

Where do Latin American men buy their **sports jackets**?

★ *at* **Sacos** *Fifth Avenue (Saks; un saco = sports jacket)*

What hats do '60s peaceniks wear when they're in Panama?

★ **jipis** *(Hippies; el jipi = Panama hat)*

FUN FACT: The "jipi" is made from the leaves of the "jipijapa" or dwarf palm tree. It was born in Jipijapa, Ecuador, and then made in Panama. It's indestructible, and a good one can hold water. Today "jipis" are made in humid caves in Becal in the Yucatán.

What Spanish film is about a man who heard a voice saying, "Open a **skirt** store, and they will come"?

★ **Falda** Dreams *(Field of Dreams; una falda = skirt)*

What did the man do after a Mexican woman in an embroidered dress bumped into him?

★ *He sued her for* **huipil**-*ash.* (whiplash; un huipil = loose-fitting blouse or sack dress with colorful embroidery across the top and bottom)

FUN FACT: The "huipil" dates to pre-Columbian times and can last thirty years. It is worn by women in the Yucatán and Central America.

What Latin American article of clothing comes from a fungus?

★ *the cami-***seta** (una camiseta = T-shirt; una seta = mushroom)

What did Edgar Allan Poe tell Mr. Von Bismarck the number on the black lace scarf's tag was?

★ *"It's the cost of the* **mantilla***, Otto."* ("The Cask of Amontillado"; una mantilla = traditional lace scarf worn by Catholic Hispanic women)

FUN FACT: The mantilla has been worn for mourning, religious processions, evening strolls, protests, and as a fashion accessory.

What do Latin American men do before buying a **suit**?

★ *They* **traje** *it on.* (un traje = suit)

What do you get when you put a Spanish father's **jacket** in the freezer?

★ *a Pop* **Saco** (Popsicle; un saco = sports coat)

What classic Leo Tolstoy novel is about a Mexican shoe?

✦ **Huarache** and Peace *(War and Peace; un huarache = sandal)*

FUN FACT: Huaraches are leather sandals worn by Mexicans. Today some are made with tire tread. In the early 1990s, Nike had a line of running shoes called "Air Huaraches." At Inca marriage ceremonies in Peru, couples exchanged sandals.

What notorious Mexican bandido wore a cape with a hole in it?

✦ ***Poncho*** Villa *(Pancho Villa; un poncho = cape with a hole in it)*

FUN FACT: The "jorongo" is another word for a poncho. Whichever word you use, you can't go "jorongo." Ponchos are a Mexican chili-coated fruit gummy candy. Pancho Villa was a notorious Mexican "Robin Hood" who achieved hero status.

What do Spanish manufacturers of ladies' shirts sing when sales are down?

✦ *They sing the **blusas**. (blues; una blusa = blouse)*

What do Mexican men wear when they eat stuffed pizza turnovers?

✦ *their calzone-cillos (unos calzoncillos = briefs, shorts)*

What do Mexicans say when their friends give them baseball **cap**s?

✦ *"Muchas **gorra**-cias." (muchas gracias; una gorra = cap)*

What Colombian superhero wears a black mask, black tights, and a **bathrobe**?

★ **Bata**-*man* (Batman; una bata = bathrobe)

Bata-man to the rescue!

Where is a coat that's hanging between a Spanish **parka** and the wall of a closet?

★ *It's between* **anorak** *and a hard place.* (a rock; un anorak = ski parka)

What do you get when you cross a Mexican **shawl** with pancakes?

★ *maple* **serape** (syrup; un serape = wool blanket coat)

What do Spanish optometrists say when they are insulted?

★ *"Is that what you think **gafas**?"* (of us; *unas gafas* = eyeglasses)

What masked hero organizes **trousers** in South American department stores?

★ *the **Pantalón** Arranger* (Lone Ranger; *un pantalón* = pair of pants)

What is the name of the famous musical about a dry cleaner from Spain?

★ Man of Las **Manchas** (Man of La Mancha = *Broadway musical of the novel* Don Quixote; *una mancha* = stain)

How high up a mountain does a Peruvian jeweler climb?

★ *as **joyas** he can go* (high as; *unas joyas* = jewelry)

What was the opening remark at the Latin American long-**sleeve**d shirt convention?

★ *"We are pleased to have you a-**manga**s."* (among us; *una manga* = sleeve)

FRUITS

Las frutas

What brand of underwear do South American **fruit** vendors wear?

★ **Fruta** the Loom *(Fruit of the Loom; una fruta = fruit)*

What do you call a fruit from Honduras that has strong views?

★ *very o-**piña**-nated (una piña = pineapple)*

FUN FACT: There are 1,600 varieties of pineapples in South America. Pineapples were growing in Honduras long before the Spanish explorers arrived.

What did the discouraged Mexican **strawberry** farmer say during the long drought?

★ *"This is very **fresa**-trating." (una fresa = strawberry)*

Why does a Spanish **grape** often get its feelings hurt?

★ *Because it's **uva**-sensitive. (over; una uva = grape)*

FUN FACT: Rumor has it the Mexican grape is uva-rated. Spanish-Mexican missionaries took the grape to California in 1564. "Uva" in Puerto Rico means "good."

What do Spanish people call a slice of **watermelon** with ice cream and chocolate sauce on it?

★ *a hot fudge **sandía** (una sandía = watermelon)*

A yummy Spanish dessert made with watermelon and ice cream.

What is the Spanish **apricot** capital of the United States?

★ ***Albaricoque**, New Mexico (Albuquerque; un albaricoque = apricot)*

What Central American tropical fruit flies passenger jets?

★ a **papaya**-lot *(pilot; una papaya = papaya)*

> **FUN FACT:** The papaya is native to Central America and southern Mexico. Mexican varieties are red or yellow, can grow to fifteen inches, and can weigh ten pounds.

Why does a South American **blackberry** expect to live forever?

★ *It believes in im-**mora**-tality. (una mora = blackberry)*

What Spanish fruit is selfish and thinks only about itself?

★ *The fig, because it has a big **higo**. (ego; un higo = fig)*

What does a Latin American **berry** farmer say when you leave?

★ *"**Baya** con Dios." (Vaya con Dios = Go with God; una baya = berry)*

What would Fred Flintstone exclaim if he were selling tropical fruit at a Mexican market?

★ *"**Guayaba** daba do!" (Yabba-dabba do; una guayaba = guava, a major fruit of Mexico)*

> **FUN FACT:** The Flintstones are "Los Picapiedra" (*Stonemasons*) in Spanish-speaking countries.

How does a Spanish **apple** grower begin fairy tales he tells his children?

★ **"Manzana**-pon a time . . ."* (once upon; una manzana = apple)

FUN FACT: "A diario una manzana es cosa sana" means "An apple a day keeps the doctor away." In Peru the custard apple or "chirimoya" grows to be as large as a human head.

Which Spanish soap opera is about adolescents who don't have cherries in their diets?

★ *"The Young and the **Cereza**-less"* (restless; una cereza = cherry)

What Bruce Springsteen hit is about a free-spirited Mexican **grapefruit** on a motorcycle?

★ *"Born **Toronja"*** ("Born to Run"; una toronja = grapefruit)

What do Latin American mathematicians get when they multiply a tropical fruit by itself?

★ ***papaya** squared* (una papaya; pi squared)

What do you call a Spanish **plum** that lives in a mansion and drives a Mercedes?

★ ***ciruela**-to-do* (well; una ciruela = plum)

What kind of pants do Colombian **grape**s wear?

★ ***uva**-ralls* (overalls; una uva = grape)

What yellow fruit swims in the swamps of South America, reaches a length of thirty feet, and peels its own skin?

★ a **banana**-conda *(una anaconda; una banana = banana)*

> **FUN FACT:** According to *Guinness World Records*, the largest bunch of bananas was grown in the Canary Islands and had 473 bananas on it.

What Spanish fruit is always calm and laid-back?

★ the *mellow-cotón (un melocotón = peach)*

What sound does a South American **coconut** make at sunrise?

★ "**Coco**-doodle-do" *(cock-a-doodle-doo; un coco = coconut)*

> **FUN FACT:** When many coconuts do it, there's quite a coco-phony. "Ser coco" is to be intelligent. "Tener buen coco" means to have a good brain.

What Spanish fruit always thinks it's being followed?

★ *The pear because it's* **pera**-*noid. (paranoid; una pera = pear)*

What are the favorite nuts of Spanish ducks?

★ *quack-ahuetes (los cacahuetes = peanuts)*

How do Spanish **blackberries** look after they've had makeovers?

★ *very gla-**moras** (una mora = blackberry)*

What principle did the Costa Rican physicist discover when he was sitting under a tropical tree and a fruit dropped on his head?

★ *the principle of* **guayaba**-*ty (gravity; una guayaba = guava)*

FUN FACT: The brand of Mexican beverages called Jarritos has a guava soda.

How the principle of guayaba-ty was discovered.

HOUSE

★

La casa

What do Latin Americans call being stuck at home all day?

★ in-**casa**-rated *(incarcerated; una casa = house)*

FUN FACT: The Feria de Alacitas (miniatures) is a South American festival for the red-nosed grinning god of the household, Ekeko. People buy statues of Ekeko and miniature versions of home gadgets and objects such as cars, hoping to get real ones in the next year.

What are the favorite chewy mints of Mexicans who rent?

★ **Aparta-Mentos** *(un apartamento = apartment)*

Why did the Spanish woman who was afraid of heights live on the lowest **floor** of tall buildings?

★ *for her* **piso** *mind (peace of; un piso = floor [level] of a building)*

On which floor of a house do Argentine sheep live?

★ *the planta baa-ja (la planta baja = ground floor of a Spanish or Latin American building)*

FUN FACT: The floors of buildings in the Hispanic world are numbered one level lower than in the United States. The ground-level floor does not have a number.

What did the satisfied Spanish woman say after the linoleum was installed in her home?

★ *"Gee, that's **suelo**." (swell; un suelo = floor)*

Why couldn't the Peruvian man find his friend's house?

★ *He lost his **dirección**. (direction; una dirección = address)*

What do Latin American people put on their faces to protect themselves from the glare of **mailbox**es?

★ ***buzón** block (sun block; un buzón = mailbox)*

What software is used to design rural Mexican homes?

★ ***Adobe** (Adobe computer software; adobe = clay used to make bricks)*

FUN FACT: Adobe bricks are made with clay, water and straw. They are stacked with mud to build homes and keep the temperature inside cool. Cactus juice is used for waterproofing.

What Disney film is about a Hawaiian girl and an alien who like to sit on Spanish **roof**s?

★ Lilo and S**techo** *(Stitch; un techo = roof)*

Where do Mexicans serve a well-known French liver appetizer?

★ *on the* **paté**-*o* *(paté = French goose liver; un patio = courtyard open to the sky)*

FUN FACT: The Spaniards introduced the patio to the Americas. It was originally a courtyard in the center of the home that provided protection. Now it's behind the house.

What do you call Latin Americans who spend a lot of time sitting in front of cafés?

★ **terraza**-*trials* *(terrestrials; una terraza = terrace)*

What does a Mexican **garden**er hope to prevent with a low-fat diet?

★ **jardín**-*ing of the arteries* *(hardening; un jardín = garden)*

What does a Spanish gardener order with a hamburger?

★ **azada** *fries* *(a side of; una azada = hoe)*

What do Mexicans call the prism's hues that come through a sunny **window**?

★ *The United Colors of* **Ventana** *(Benetton; una ventana = window)*

What Spanish TV sitcom is about a family's great affection for a black **window grate**?

★ *"Everybody Loves **Reja**"* (Ray[mond]; una reja = wrought iron window grate)

   FUN FACT: The "reja" is a decorative element of architecture that was brought to the Americas by the Spaniards.

What do you get when you cross a New York airport and a Mexican **attic**?

★ *La **Guardilla*** (La Guardia; una guardilla = attic)

What rooms of a Spanish house go great with milk?

★ *the dormit-Oreos* (un dormitorio = bedroom)

What room of a South American house keeps pulling you back again and again?

★ *the **cuarto de baño**-yo* (yoyo; un cuarto de baño = bathroom)

What did the Mexican man say as he sat by himself in his **living room**?

★ *"I'm **salón**-ly."* (so lonely; un salón = living room)

What female friend of Hercules fights warlords and lives in a Spanish **kitchen**?

★ ***Cocina**, the Princess Warrior* (Xena; una cocina = kitchen)

What male '70s group sang in **dining rooms** all over Latin America?

★ The **Comedores** *(Commodores; un comedor = dining room)*

What small cars are manufactured in two minutes in Spain?

★ *micro-Hondas (un microondas = microwave oven)*

> **FUN FACT:** The SEAT is a make of Spanish car. Among its models are the Ibiza, the León, and the Altea.

What do you get when you cross Albert Einstein with a Spanish **clock**maker?

★ *the theory of **reloj**-tivity (el reloj = clock)*

Why couldn't the Puerto Rican woman fry her eggs?

★ *She was un-**sartén** about which pan to use. (uncertain; un sartén = frying pan)*

What Mexican **oven** repairman tells people he'll be back?

★ **Horno** *Schwarzenegger (Arnold; un horno = oven)*

How do Mexican pots greet each other?

★ *¡**Olla**! (¡Hola!; una olla = round earthenware pot)*

What did Edgar Allan Poe's raven say as it sat on top of the Spanish **refrigerator**?

★ *"**Nevera** more."* ("Nevermore"; una nevera = refrigerator)

Quoth the Spanish raven on the fridge, "¡Nevera more!"

What breed of dog does the laundry in South American homes?

★ a **Lavadora** Retriever (Labrador; una lavadora = washing machine)

What do Mexican chefs say to welcome each other into their kitchens?

★ *"Mi **cazo** es su cazo."* (Mi casa es su casa = My house is your house; un cazo = saucepan)

FUN FACT: "Mi casa es su casa" means "Make yourself at home." In Mexico a teen slang word for house is "la cueva" or "cave."

Who is crowned each year in a Latin American furniture store?

★ **Mesa**-*merica* *(Miss America; una mesa = table)*

> **FUN FACT:** "¡A la mesa!" means "Come and get it," "Soup's on," or "Dinner's ready."

Where do Spanish people buy their **chairs**?

★ *at* **Sillas** *Roebuck (Sears; una silla = chair)*

> **FUN FACT:** There are eight Sears Roebuck stores in Mexico City.

What Mexican TV sitcom is about a bed stuck between two other **bed**s in a dysfunctional household?

★ *"Mal-***cama** *in the Middle" (Malcolm; una cama = bed)*

> **FUN FACT:** Frankie (Francisco) Muñoz, who plays the title character in the zany TV show "Malcolm in the Middle," has a Puerto Rican father and an Irish mother. He learned to play golf when he was five, had many parts in local theater productions, plays the drums, and wants to be a race car driver. He starred in *Agent Cody Banks* and its sequel.

What is the favorite pasta dish of Mexicans who sleep on suspended woven nets?

★ **hamaca**-*roni and cheese (una hamaca = hammock)*

> **FUN FACT:** You can buy hammocks in Mexico at Hamaca-Schlemmer (Hammacher). Mérida in the Yucatán is a major center of hammock production.

Who creates dance routines for Spanish goldfish?

★ an **acuario**-*grapher* (choreographer; un acuario = aquarium)

The Spanish acuario-grapher teaches a new "fish-hop" dance.

What do Mexicans call the speed with which a **candle** burns?

★ its **vela**-*city* (velocity; una vela = candle)

What statistic tells how many **armchair**s there are in Spain?

★ the popula-**sillón** (population; un sillón = armchair)

What Greek philosopher was inspired sitting on a Spanish **couch**?

★ **Sofá**-*cles* (Sophocles; un sofá = couch)

What do Latin Americans call it when two sofa **cushion**s look the same?

★ *a **cojín**-cidence (coincidence; un cojin = cushion)*

In what store do Latin Americans buy **wall-to-wall carpeting**?

★ *a super-**moqueta** (supermarket; la moqueta = wall-to-wall carpeting)*

Why did María put her sweater in her pajama **drawer**?

★ *She got **cajón**-fused. (confused; un cajón = drawer)*

What does the red "Sesame Street" puppet rest his head on at night?

★ *an Elmo-hada (una almohada = pillow)*

FUN FACT: In 1978 Luis Santeiro was the first Hispanic to work for "Calle Sésamo." "Consultar con la almohada" (consult with the pillow) means "to sleep on it."

What did Sherlock Holmes say to his assistant when he solved the "Case of the Missing Mexican **Blanket**"?

★ *"It's ele-**manta**-ry, my dear Watson." (una manta = blanket)*

What was the Spanish husband's reaction to the French **bedspread** his wife bought?

★ *He had **colcha** shock. (culture; una colcha = bedspread)*

Who was the top **blanket** salesman of the Aztec empire?

★ ***Manta***-*zuma (Montezuma = Aztec chief; una manta = blanket)*

FUN FACT: Montezuma (1466–1520) drank from forty to fifty goblets of chocolate a day. His mistake was giving Hernán Cortés luxurious parting gifts. Cortés saw all the gold and decided to stay. That led to the destruction of the Aztec empire.

Manta-zuma was the Aztec's top blanket salesman.

At which convenience store do Latin American people buy **sheet**s?

★ *at **Sábana**-Eleven (7-Eleven; una sábana = sheet)*

What is a Spanish bathroom **sink** like?

★ *It's very **lavabo**. (lovable; un lavabo = sink)*

What kind of sunglasses do Latin Americans wear in a **bathtub**?

★ Ray-**Bañera** *(Ray-Ban; una bañera = bathtub)*

What play did the Spanish Shakespeare write in the **shower**?

★ Much A-**ducha** About Nothing *(Ado; una ducha = shower)*

What do Spanish children say when they line up to race to the **bathroom**?

★ "**Baño** mark, get set, go!" *(On your; un baño = bathroom)*

What do South Americans call it when a **bed** blends in with the decor of a room?

★ **cama**-flage *(camouflage; una cama = bed)*

Cama-flage is the latest trend in South American bedroom decor.

What did the Peanuts character Lucy say about
the **faucet** that her friend installed in the Spanish
bathroom?

★ *"Good **grifo**, Charlie Brown."* *(un grifo = faucet)*

FUN FACT: "¡Qué bárbaro!" is "Good grief!" In Spain, Charlie
is Carlitos, Rerun is Bis, and Woodstock is Emilio. "C" on Mexican
faucets is for "caliente" (hot), not "cold."

MEXICO

★

¡Viva México!

What Mexican river makes people grumble?

★ *the Río Groan-de (Río Grande)*

   FUN FACT: The Río Grande makes up two-thirds of the 2,000-mile-long border between the United States and Mexico. The river is the southern border of Texas.

What are cats from south of the border doing when they leap around the yard?

★ *the Mexican Cat Prance (Mexican Hat Dance = national dance of Mexico)*

   FUN FACT: The Mexican Hat Dance (Jarabe Tapatío) from the state of Jalisco is a courting dance. A man throws his hat on the floor and the couple dances around it, flirting. When the man wins her heart, the woman picks up the hat and puts it on her head.

Where do customers at a supermarket in Guadalajara wait to check out?

★ *in a Mexi-**cola*** *(Mexico = los Estados Unidos Mexicanos; una cola = line)*

FUN FACT: Mexico (Méjico) means "navel of the moon." It has thirty-one states and its capital is México, D.F. (Distrito Federal).

What do you call a man from a northwest region of Mexico who makes noise when he sleeps?

★ *a **sonora*** *(snorer; Sonora = state in northwestern Mexico)*

FUN FACT: Sonora is called the "Wild West" of Mexico. The desert in Sonora has more than 300 species of cactus plants. El Pinacate, a volcano preserve, has 600 volcanic craters.

What is a cross between Burger King and a northern Mexican city with the name of a dog?

★ *a Chihua-huapper (Whopper; Chihuahua = state of Mexico on the U.S. border)*

FUN FACT: Chihuahua (dry, sandy place) has seven border crossings and 360 "maquiladoras" or foreign assembly plants. Chihuahua has waterfalls, deserts, and the magnificent Copper Canyon, which is as big as several Grand Canyons.

Where do people from a Mexican Pacific resort town sell their antiques and unwanted household items?

★ *at a **Puerto Vallarta** sale (yard sale; Puerto Vallarta = town on the west coast)*

What is the most common men's hair style in southern Mexico?

★ *the Mo-Oaxaca* *(Mohawk; Oaxaca = southern Mexican state and its capital)*

FUN FACT: Oaxaca, Náhuatl for "in the nose of the squash," has many archaeological sites. It's a paradise of colorful folk art and handicrafts. Puerto Escondido hosts world surfing championships. The famous Mexican Pipeline is a huge wave for advanced surfers.

What breed of Mexican dog is pink and erupts into fits of barking?

★ *the Popocaté-poodle* *(Popocatépetl = "smoking mountain" volcano)*

FUN FACT: Popocatépetl is near Mexico City. It erupted in 1997 and 2001 and is the country's second highest peak. "Popo" watches over its legendary lady friend volcano, the nearby Iztaccíhuatl (Izta).

Where in Mexico do people walk like ducks?

★ *in Waddle-ahara* *(Guadalajara = Mexico's second largest city)*

FUN FACT: Guadalajara is the capital of Jalisco. It's home to the mariachis, rodeos (charreadas), tequila, the sombrero, and the Mexican Hat Dance.

What are the bridesmaids at a pig's **wedding** in Tijuana called?

★ *sows of the **boda*** *(south of the border; una boda = wedding)*

FUN FACT: Tijuana is the busiest border crossing between Mexico and the United States. It is fifteen miles away from San Diego.

Sows of the boda chat before a Tijuana wedding.

What Mexican state manufactures equipment for soaking in spas?

★ *Hot Tubasco* *(hot tub; Tabasco = state in southern Mexico on the coast)*

FUN FACT: Tabasco (waterlogged, humid earth) produces oil, cacao, bananas, and sugarcane. Tabasco sauce, made from hot peppers, is not from Tabasco but is made in Louisiana. Tabasco has 1,000 archaeological sites.

What magazine is devoted to the construction of Mexican beach **shelter**s?

★ **Palapa** Mechanics *(Popular; una palapa = beach shelter with a thatched roof)*

> **FUN FACT:** A "palapa" is made with four poles and has a roof made of palm fronds. People sit under it for shade. The next time you're on a Mexican beach, "palapa" chair and relax under a "palapa."

What do tourists get when they lie on beaches in Cancún?

★ a **Yuca-tan** *(Yucatán = state and peninsula in southern Mexico)*

> **FUN FACT:** The Yucatán Peninsula is rich in Mayan history with ruins such as Chichén Itzá and Uxmal. The gorgeous Mayan Riviera is on the Caribbean coast of the Yucatán.

What warning did the teacher from the Mayan city give the parents of the boy who was suspected of copying answers from another student's test?

★ *"He cheats and it's a zero."* *(Chitzén Itzá = Mayan city)*

> **FUN FACT:** Chitzén Itzá was the religious capital of the Mayan civilization from 800 to 1400 A.D. It is dominated by the steep 79-foot pyramid of Kukulcán (El Castillo) and has sacred temples and the largest ball court found at any Mayan ruins.

What Mexican Indian model from the Sierra Madre Mountains runs down the catwalk?

★ *Tyrahumara Banks* *(Tyra Banks; Tarahumara Indians from Chihuahua)*

FUN FACT: The Tarahumara Indians of the Copper Canyon in the Sierra Madre mountains are the world's best long distance runners, running fifty to seventy miles a day. They've been known to run 170 miles without stopping . . . and in sandals.

What does a Mexican scrooge from Cabo San Lucas say?

★ **"Baja** *humbug."* *(Bah; Baja California = state of Mexico on a long peninsula)*

FUN FACT: Baja California, the largest peninsula in the world, is 1,100 miles long, and extends from Tijuana to Los Cabos. It is mostly desert with miles of isolated beaches. Scenes from the film *Titanic* were filmed on a Baja beach, where a replica of the ship was built.

At what famous Mexican resort do people from Poland spend their vacations?

★ *Acapolaco* *(Acapulco = Pacific coast town; polaco = Polish)*

FUN FACT: Acapulco is a paradise resort on a rounded bay with over a dozen beaches. It's called the "Pearl of the Pacific." The first disco in North America was in Acapulco. Acapulco is home to the famous daring cliff divers.

What kind of movie about pottery scares people from Jalisco?

★ *a Guadala-horror story (Guadalajara = capital of the state of Jalisco)*

FUN FACT: Guadalajara has a huge handicrafts center with over 10,000 artisans creating souvenirs that are "hechos en México" (made in Mexico). The Mercado Libertad is Latin America's largest indoor mall with 1,000 vendors.

What was the nickname of the Mayan ruler from Palenque who loved to play ice hockey?

★ *King Puck-al (Pakal = king of the Maya who ruled Palenque for eighty years)*

FUN FACT: The tomb of King Pakal was discovered in 1952 at the Palenque ruins, eighty-two feet beneath a pyramid. Pakal was wearing a jade death mask and had a jade ring on each finger. He was a mean ruler. He made people walk the Palenque (plank)!

What Mexican-American singer is a **legend** in her own time?

★ **Leyenda** *Ronstadt (Linda; una leyenda = legend)*

FUN FACT: Linda Rondstadt's hits include "Different Drum," "When Will I Be Loved," "You're No Good," and "Blue Bayou." Her father was of Mexican and German descent. She recorded an album called "Canciones de mi padre."

What do tourists who have white moustaches at Mexico City's floating gardens say?

★ *"Got **Xochimilco?**"* (milk; Xochimilco = floating gardens near Mexico City)

FUN FACT: The Aztecs created 15,000 "floating gardens" or "chinampas" on Lake Texcoco. Today only 1,500 of them are left. Tourists ride in flower-decorated boats called "trajineras."

What do people from southern Mexico put on their lips when they're dry?

★ ***Chiapas** Stick* (Chap Stick; Chiapas = state that borders on Guatemala)

FUN FACT: Chiapas has the largest tropical forest in Mexico with 10,000 species of plants. It's a region of many Mayan ruins. Chiapas is famous for its weavers.

What is the TV game show that gives Mexican Indians inheritances as prizes for answering a series of questions?

★ *"Who Wants to Be a **Maya**n Heir?"* (Millionaire; Maya = Indians of southern Mexico and Central America)

FUN FACT: The Maya domesticated the dog. There are descendants of the Maya in southern Mexico today.

Where in Mexico do French dancers go for their vacations?

★ *to Cancan-cún (Cancún = resort on the Yucatán peninsula)*

FUN FACT: Cancún was created by the Mexican government in the 1970s. Over fifty hotels line the shore with beaches of soft white sand. People ride on inflated banana boats in the crystal clear turquoise ocean. ¡Magnífico!

What did the Mexican cliff diver say about a fellow diver?

★ *"He's **La Quebrada**." (like a brother; La Quebrada = cliff in Acapulco)*

FUN FACT: The divers (clavadistas) at La Quebrada jump from 140-foot cliffs, landing in 15 feet of water below. They carry torches in the evening on the last two dives of the day.

What do you call a person who pretends to be from a popular Baja border town?

★ *a Ti-wannabe (Tijuana = Mexican border town eighteen miles from San Diego)*

FUN FACT: Tijuana is named after a cantina owner, Tía Juana (Aunt Jane). The city has a Museo de Cera (Wax Museum) with eighty figures including Bill Cosby, Elvis Presley, Emiliano Zapata, Madonna, Dracula, John Lennon, and Ghandi.

What did Mexican Indians from Chichén Itzá put in their egg salad?

★ *Mayan-esa (la mayonesa = mayonnaise)*

FUN FACT: Mayonnaise came from Mahón on the island of Menorca off the coast of Spain. The sauce, called "mahonesa," was taken to France and became a culinary hit.

What do Mexicans call singers, dancers, comedians, and actors from the United States?

★ *en-**norte**-ners (entertainers; El Norte = the United States)*

FUN FACT: "Americano" means anyone from North, Central, or South America. So, "Soy norteamericano" (not "Soy americano") is the correct way to say you're from the United States.

What do you get when you cross Mr. Afleck and Mr. Stiller on pogo sticks in Guadalajara?

★ *Mexican Jumping Bens (beans)*

FUN FACT: Álamos is the "frijoles saltarines" capital. The jumping beans, however, are not beans but seeds that come from a shrub. Butterflies or moths inject larvae into the seeds and coat them shut. When the larvae become caterpillars, they try to escape and bounce off the seed walls. That's what causes the "jumping."

Why does the Mexican woman want to quit her job?

★ *Because the **peso** low. (pay's so; un peso = Mexican unit of money)*

FUN FACT: The peso is worth about ten cents. "Te falta cinco para el peso" means "you're not playing with a full deck."

What do Mexicans use after brushing their teeth that makes them laugh?

★ *Cantin-floss* *(Cantinflas = beloved Mexican comedian and actor)*

FUN FACT: Mario Moreno Reyes (1911–1993) was a boxer, dancer, circus performer, comedian, and actor who made fifty films. He is best known as his clown character, Cantinflas. He made people laugh with his hilarious plays on language. Charlie Chaplin admired him greatly. There is a statue of Cantinflas in Mexico City.

What do Mexicans shout when they see five English speakers in a horizontal, vertical, or diagonal line?

★ **"Gringo."** *(Bingo; un[a] gringo[a] = English speaker, a U.S. citizen, foreigner)*

FUN FACT: "Gringo" means foreigner and refers to people from the United States. It used to be an insult, but its connotation has mellowed. Scholars say it's from "griego," or "Greek," and meant "jibberish," as in "That's Greek to me." They dispel the theory that it came about when Mexicans heard U.S. soldiers singing "Green Grow the Rushes" during the Mexican-American War (1846–1848).

What Mexican store sells colorful percussion instruments that you shake?

★ *Neiman **Maracas*** *(Neiman Marcus; una maraca = dried gourd with seeds in it)*

FUN FACT: Maracas are also made of wood or plastic and painted with colorful images.

What do strolling Mexican musicians put on their nachos?

★ *mariacheese (los mariachis = strolling musicians originally from Jalisco)*

FUN FACT: "Mariachis" wear black shirts, bolero jackets, and wide-brimmed hats. They play trumpets, violins, and guitars and sing about romance, heroes, and macho themes. "Cielito Lindo" and "La Cucaracha" are two classic mariachi songs.

What do Grammy-winning Mexican guitarists put on their skin at the beach?

★ *Santana lotion (suntan; Carlos Santana = recording artist from Mexico)*

FUN FACT: Santana, the first Latin rock band in the United States, was started by Carlos Santana in 1968. "Oye Como Va" and "Black Magic Woman" were huge hits, and Santana won nine Grammys. The album *Supernatural* made Carlos a sensation again in 2000.

What was the favorite coffee of the Mayan rain god?

★ **Chaac** *Full of Nuts (Chock; Chaac = Mayan god of rain, thunder, fertility, and agriculture)*

FUN FACT: Chaac lived at the bottom of a cenote, or well, which is why he is drawn with amphibian traits and is linked to frogs. When a human sacrifice was made, Chaac rose into the sky and scratched the clouds to make it ran. He carried an ax that made thunder.

What line does Smokey Robinson sing to a Mexican agave plant?

★ **"Maguey**, *maguey. Talkin' 'bout maguey."* *("My Girl"; un maguey = agave plant)*

FUN FACT: The maguey plant grows in Mexico and is used to make cloth, paper, and rope. The phrase "Okei, maguey" is like the English word "Okeydoke."

What does a Mexican gum salesman ask his wife when he comes home from work?

★ *"What's for **sapodilla**?"* *(supper, dear; una sapodilla = gum tree)*

FUN FACT: The sapodilla tree produces a substance from which chewing gum (el chicle) is made. Mexican children sell small square "chiclets" in the streets. The Aztecs chewed "chicle" to freshen their breath.

What do **silver** vendors from Taxco need when they act conceited about their jewelry?

★ *a **plata**-tude adjustment (attitude; la plata = silver)*

FUN FACT: Taxco has white buildings with red roofs and 300 "platerías" or silver shops. Taxco was the very first mining town in the Americas.

What did early Mexican Indian stockbrokers check in the financial pages every day?

★ *the NAZTEC Index (Aztec; NAZDAQ)*

Why can't the Mexican boy eat **cactus**?

★ *He is **cactos**-intolerant.* (lactose; un cacto = cactus)

FUN FACT: There are 1,600 varieties of cacti in Mexico. The tallest cactus recorded is the Cardón cactus in the Sonora Desert in Baja, California. It's 63 feet tall. Oaxacans eat fried cactus.

What is the name of Mexico's ballet company of **seal**s?

★ *the Ballet **Foca**lórico* (Ballet Folklórico = national dance company; una foca = seal)

FUN FACT: The Ballet Folklórico de México was founded in 1950. It tours the world, presenting colorful dances and music from Mexico's culture and history.

What did the archaeologist say to his friend as they shared the relics they found in southern Mexico?

★ *"What's yours is yours and what's **Maya**n is mine."*

FUN FACT: The Maya thought that crossed eyes were attractive. They hung gadgets on strings in front of their faces to train their eyes to cross.

What did Otis Redding sing to a Mexican **cactus**?

★ *"Sittin' on the Dock of **Agave**."* (Bay; un agave = aloe plant)

FUN FACT: The agave (maguey) is used to make rope and string for weaving. Raw agave is poisonous. The agave has tall stalks with flowers on them.

What did the Aztec say when he climbed to the top of the steep pyramid and was afraid to climb back down?

★ **"Náhuatl** I do?" *(Now what'll; Náhuatl = language of the Aztecs)*

FUN FACT: Náhuatl is still spoken in the Yucatán Peninsula and in Chiapas. Some words in Náhuatl are: tomatl (tomato), ayotl (turtle), chokolatl (chocolate), elotl (corn), koyotl (coyote), and xochitl (flower).

What city do you get when you cross Popeye and the Aztecs?

★ *Spinach-titlán (Tenochtitlán = Aztec capital from 1325 to 1521)*

FUN FACT: After the Aztecs saw a sign from the gods—an eagle on a cactus with a snake in its talons—on an island in Lake Texcoco, they buit their capital city, Tenochtitlán. Two hundred years later, Hernán Cortés destroyed the city. Mexico City was built on the ruins of Tenochtitlán.

What do some women from a Mexican Gulf Coast port have on the back of their legs?

★ **Veracruz** veins *(varicose; Veracruz = state and city on the Mexican Gulf Coast)*

FUN FACT: Veracruz is known for orchids. Roberto Ávila, who played for the Cleveland Indians, was a governor of Veracruz. The Ritchie Valens song "La Bamba" is about the ransacking of Veracruz in 1683 by a Dutch pirate and his men.

What would a person from a southern Mexico state be doing if it snowed there?

★ ***Oaxacan*** *in a winter wonderland (Walking; Oaxaca = southern Mexican state)*

FUN FACT: Oaxacans eat grasshoppers or "chapulines." They are boiled with garlic and spices, smoked, sautéed with butter, roasted, fried with chile, fried with garlic and lime, or served with warm tortillas.

What did the two Mayan Indians say when they realized they were from the same village?

★ *"It's* ***Uxmal*** *world." (small; Uxmal = Mayan ruins in the Yucatán)*

FUN FACT: Uxmal means "three times built." Its largest pyramid is the Pyramid of the Magician. It was supposedly built in one night, a task that saved a boy's life and made him the new ruler.

RESTAURANT

★

EL restaurante

Where do peace-loving reggae fans eat when they're in Spain?

★ *in rasta-rantes (Rasta; un restaurante = restaurant)*

FUN FACT: Some restaurants in Spain are "casas de comida" (eating houses), "tascas" (appetizer taverns), and "cafés." Mexico has "cantinas," "loncherías," "snack-bares," "fondas" (inns), and "cafeterías."

What do Latin American waiters use to write **lunch** orders?

★ ***almuerzo** code (Morse Code; un almuerzo = lunch)*

FUN FACT: *Guinness World Records* says that the fastest restaurant service time in Mexico is 13.5 seconds. The Karne Garibaldi in Jalisco has only one item on the menu—"carne en su jugo"—which is practically served when you walk in the door.

What is the Spanish woman doing when she bangs pots and pans in the kitchen?

★ *making a big* **cena** *(scene; una cena = dinner)*

> **FUN FACT:** Dinner in the Spanish-speaking world is eaten any time between 9:00 P.M. and 11:00 P.M. While eating dinner, Spaniards often watch cable news on CNN. (¡Cenan! Groan!)

What do you get when you cross "Proud Mary" and a Mexican restaurant?

★ *Ike* **cantina** *Turner (Ika and Tina; una cantina = traditional Mexican bar)*

> **FUN FACT:** The cantina began as a separate room of a restaurant that was exclusively for men. Today many cantinas have opened up to women.

What Disney cartoon couple moonlights as waiters in Spain?

★ *Mickey* **Mozo** *and Minnie* **Moza** *(Mouse; un mozo = male waiter; una moza = female waiter)*

What car does a male Spanish restaurant employee drive?

★ *a* **Camarero** *(Camaro; un camarero = male waiter)*

> **FUN FACT:** When paying in Mexican restaurants, customers should put the money or credit card right into the server's hand. Leaving it on the table is rude and insulting.

When were Spanish **table**s invented?

★ *during the **Mesa**-zoic era (Mezozoic; una mesa = table)*

FUN FACT: A mesa is a flat-topped geological elevation. Some table makers in Spain are depressed because they're mesa-understood.

How does a Mexican **tablecloth** know that you're going to buy it?

★ *It has **mantel** telepathy. (mental; un mantel = tablecloth)*

What is a Spanish **spoon** that shouts "Go, Fight, Win"?

★ *a **cuchara** leader (cheerleader; una cuchara = spoon)*

What Brazilian dance do South Americans do when they drink out of a **glass**?

★ *the **vaso**-nova (bossanova; un vaso = glass)*

What dance do people at Spanish restaurants do after eating an **appetizer**?

★ *a **tapa** dance (a tap dance; una tapa = Spanish appetizer sold in special eateries)*

FUN FACT: "Tapas" are small appetizers served at "tabernas" or "tascas" in the late afternoon/early evening. In the thirteenth century, King Alfonso X's doctor told him to eat small snacks. This is one theory of the origin of "tapas."

Where are Spanish people sitting when they eat an **appetizer** in a café?

★ *They're sittin' on **tapa** the world.* (on top of; una tapa = appetizer)

FUN FACT: "Tapa" means "lid." Bartenders would put small plates on wineglasses to keep the flies away. Small appetizers were put on the dishes.

What do Spanish restaurants use to store leftover **appetizer**s?

★ ***Tapa**ware* (Tupperware; las tapas = hot or cold Spanish appetizers)

FUN FACT: "Tapas" ingredients include olives, sausages, quail, meatballs, eggs, fish, calamari, beef tongue, and octopus. "Tapear" means to go from "tapas" bar to "tapas" bar, snacking and socializing with people before going home.

What four letters refer to a well-done Spanish steak?

★ *B.N.H.O.* (bien hecho = well-done)

What part of a Spanish meal makes suds?

★ *the **sopa*** (soap; una sopa = soup)

FUN FACT: The Mexicans have a "dry soup" called "sopa seca." An ingredient such as pasta or rice soaks up all the liquid.

What do Mexican chip lovers get when they warm their feet by the fireplace?

★ *toasty toes* (Tostitos)

What is the favorite soup of Spanish dogs?

★ *gaz-poocho (el gazpacho = cold tomato soup from Spain)*

FUN FACT: Gazpacho is like a salad you can drink. It's made with tomatoes, spices, cucumbers, onions, and olive oil. There are forty red, green, or white variations. Gazpacho used to be a "pauper's soup," made with only water, olive oil, and bread.

What is a Mexican duck's favorite dip?

★ *quackamole (guacamole = dip made with avocados, tomatoes, lime juice, onions, and chile)*

What Austrian city is the best place for dipping Mexican tortilla chips?

★ **Salsa**-*burg (Salzburg)*

FUN FACT: Salsa is a Mexican sauce and topping for many dishes. It's made with diced tomatoes, chile peppers, onions, and other ingredients such as avocado, mango, peaches, black beans, and even cactus.

What do you get when you cross Hawaiian dancers and hot Mexican peppers?

★ *hula-peños (un jalapeño = hot pepper named after Jalapa, Veracruz)*

FUN FACT: The International Federation of Competitive Eating says that Jed Donahue ate 152 jalapeños in fifteen minutes in 2002. A jalapeño jelly is made in Texas.

How do Mexican **pepper** growers communicate?

★ *by **chile**-mail (e-mail)*

> **FUN FACT:** Chiles are red, green, or yellow. There are 150 varieties of chiles in Mexico. The "cascabel" chile looks like a small bell and its seeds seem to jingle.

What did the Mexican shopper shout when a man ran off with the cheddar from her shopping cart?

★ *"Hey, that's **nacho** cheese!" (That's not your; los nachos = tortilla chips covered with melted cheese and chiles)*

> **FUN FACT:** Some Spanish supermarkets are El Corte Inglés, Alcampo, Hipercor, and Caprabo. Some Mexican supermarkets are Comercial Mexicana, Gigante, Soriana, and Aurrerá. Nachos with melted cheese are not authentic Mexican appetizers.

What do you get when you cross Willie Wonka and a Mexican-style layered appetizer?

★ *Johnny Nine-Layer Depp (Nine-Layer Dip = appetizer with Mexican-style ingredients)*

What do you call a video about making Mexican flat bread that makes people cry?

★ *a real **tortilla** jerker (una tortilla = Mexican bread)*

> **FUN FACT:** The Mexican tortilla was made of "masa" (corn dough) for centuries. Mexican workers couldn't find "masa" in the United States, so they made flour tortillas. The soft tortillas were filled with meat and beans and rolled up, and the burrito was born.

What would a princess of Mexican bread wear on her head?

★ *a **tortilla**-ara (tiara; una tortilla = thin round of corn or flour)*

> **FUN FACT:** In Spain a tortilla is something different. It's an omelette. It may have potatoes, onions, artichokes, mushrooms, ham, asparagus, or cheese in it.

What happened to the Mexican tortilla maker who didn't use the right flour?

★ *He was charged with a **masa**-demeanor. (la masa = corn dough or flour)*

What happened when all the Mexican stores ran out of cornmeal flour?

★ *There was **masa** hysteria. (la masa = corn dough or flour)*

How do Mexicans pay for corn flour?

★ *with their **Masa**-ter Card (Master Card)*

What giggling toy do you get when you cross "Sesame Street" with a Mexican food?

★ ***Taco** Me Elmo (Tickle Me Elmo)*

> **FUN FACT:** Tacos are sold from carts or "taquerías" (taco stands). Fish tacos are eaten on the Baja peninsula. Some Mexicans like grasshopper tacos.

What is it called when two people are pulling the opposite ends of a folded Mexican tortilla?

★ a **taco** war *(tug-of-war)*

> **FUN FACT:** According to *Guinness World Records*, the largest taco was 36 feet long. It weighed 1,654 pounds and contained 182 pounds of steak. It was prepared for the centennial celebration of Mexicali, Baja California.

What is the science of making folded Mexican tortillas?

★ **taco**-nology *(technology; un taco)*

> **FUN FACT:** "Los tacos" is slang in Mexico for "bad words."

Why wasn't the Mexican lawyer allowed to open a restaurant?

★ He didn't pass the bar-rito exam. *(bar; un burrito = meat and beans folded in a tortilla)*

> **FUN FACT:** "Burrito," meaning "little donkey," wasn't originally a Spanish word for something to eat. It was invented by Americans in the last century and refers to the folded tacos Mexicans sold on their donkeys at the border. What we call a taco is a burrito in Mexico.

What did the Tex-Mex chef reply when asked if he was quitting the cooking contest?

★ "No. I have not yet begun to **fajita**." *(to fight; las fajitas = grilled meat on a tortilla)*

Which actor from "The West Wing" likes deep-fried burritos?

★ **Chimichanga** Smits *(Jimmy Smits; una chimichanga = deep-fried burrito)*

FUN FACT: The "chimichanga" is a crispy burrito. It was born one day when a burrito accidentally fell into a deep fryer at an Arizona restaurant.

Where do Tex-Mex grill cooks work out?

★ in **fajita**-ness centers *(fitness; las fajitas = Tex-Mex dish of sizzling grilled steak, tortillas, and typical Mexican toppings)*

FUN FACT: "Fajita" means "little girdle" or "belt." The self-proclaimed "Fajita King" is Sonny Falcon of Texas. Mexican ranch workers in the southwest United States are credited with inventing the fajita. They turned the scraps of beef their bosses gave them into fajitas.

What did the Tex-Mex chef say after standing up all day grilling strips of beef?

★ "My **fajita** killing me." *(feet are; una fajita)*

What Mexican dish is a beautiful blue-green color?

★ a tur-**quesadilla** *(turquesa = turquoise; quesadilla = two-tortilla grilled "sandwich" with cheese inside)*

FUN FACT: The word "queso" (cheese) is the root of the word "quesadilla." Quesadillas are cut into wedges. A "sincronizada" is a quesadilla with two ingredients, such as cheese with chicken or ham.

What does the star of the musical "Annie" sing in Mexico?

★ *"The sun'll come out **tamale**"* *(tomorrow; un tamal = filled and steamed Mexican snack)*

FUN FACT: Tamales, invented 5,000 years ago, are a common breakfast food sold by Mexican street vendors. Masa dough is filled and then wrapped in corn husks, tied, and steamed. Banana leaves are also used.

What Mexican señorita likes to soak at the spa while eating corn husk snacks?

★ *Hot Tub Molly* *(hot tamale)*

FUN FACT: A pan for steaming "tamales" is called a "tamalera." It was proper etiquette for the Aztecs to hold tamales in their left hands. They made frog, turkey, and pocket gopher tamales. Tamales were offered to the gods.

What do people take for indigestion after eating a traditional Mexican **sauce**?

★ *Pepto Bis-**mole**** *(Pepto-Bismol; el mole = chocolate sauce with spices)*

FUN FACT: The Aztec chief Montezuma liked "mole poblano," made with the dark-green "poblano" pepper and served on turkey. When tourists eat fresh produce that isn't washed well, they might get the dreaded "Montezuma's revenge."

What hot beverage does Jerry Seinfeld drink when he's in Spain with his neighbor?

★ ***café** con Kremer* *(el café con crema = coffee with cream)*

What do Mexican **sauce** chefs hear when they log onto their Internet service?

★ *"You've got **mole**."* (mail; el mole = Mexican sauce or gravy made with chocolate)

FUN FACT: "Mole" is made with sesame seeds, nuts, chocolate, spices, dried chiles, corn dough, dried fruits, and vegetables. It's red, yellow, green, black, or brown. Mole is typically served with chicken, beef, or pork.

Claudio, the Mexican chef, goes online.

What kind of spicy candy does the Easter Bunny bring to Mexican children?

★ **chile** beans (Jelly beans; un chile = pepper)

What did the Mexican woman say when her friend suggested they order a coconut drink?

★ *"**Atole** agree."* (I totally; el atole = beverage with masa dough with coconut and walnut flavoring)

What do you get when you cross a Mexican **meatball** with Agent 007?

★ **Albóndiga**. *James Albóndiga. (Bond; una albóndiga = meatball)*

What orange seafood and rice dish is served in Valencia on Halloween?

★ *pumpkin **paella** (pumpkin pie; la paella = rice, seafood, and saffron dish from Valencia, Spain)*

FUN FACT: There are hundreds of "paella" recipes that vary from yellow to black. Black paellas are colored with squid ink. "Paellas" are served at "arrocerías" (rice dish restaurants) and other restaurants.

What do you call the sound a Spanish rice and seafood dish makes while it's cooking?

★ *onomato-**paella** (onomatopoeia; la paella = rice dish from Valencia)*

FUN FACT: A "paellera" is a shallow black paella skillet. In some villages, "paelleras" are outside and are as big as hot tubs. Though squirrel paella is now banned, paellas are made in some regions with rat and rabbit meat.

What does a Spanish child who's excited about eating a **roll** say?

★ *"Oh, **bollo** boy." (boy oh boy; un bollo = roll)*

FUN FACT: In Spain you can find rolls with chocolate morsels (pepitas de chocolate) in them.

What can you say about the Spanish chef who can prepare **turnover**s with very few ingredients?

★ *He makes **empanada** nothing. (something out of; una empanada = filled turnover in the shape of a semicircle)*

FUN FACT: "Empanadas" are small turnovers filled with meat, seafood, chicken, or fruit. In Mexico, empanadas are mostly desserts, filled with pumpkin, sweet potato, or fruits.

What did the server say when Pepe asked when his **burger** would be ready?

★ *"Your **hamburguesa**'s good as mine." (guess is as; una hamburguesa = hamburger)*

FUN FACT: McDonald's "McMenú" in Spain sells McMarins de pescado (fish sticks), McNuggets de pollo (Chicken McNuggets), the Cuarto de libra con queso (Quarter Pounder with Cheese), the McPollo, the McRoyal Deluxe, the Big Mac, and the Big Big Mac.

How do Mexican servers indicate on an order that two people want the same sandwich?

★ *They use empare-ditto marks. (ditto; un emparedado = sandwich)*

FUN FACT: "Un bocadillo" is a sandwich in Spain with ham, tuna, sausage, veal, Manchego cheese, or steak. Pans and Company is a sandwich-shop chain in Spain.

What do Spanish cows call being **milked** when they want to be?

★ ***leche** faire (laissez faire; la leche = milk)*

What do you call a Spanish deep-fried dough stick that is undercooked?

★ *an imma-**churro*** *(immature; un churro = long tube-like fried pastry)*

> **FUN FACT:** "Churros," long fritters from Spain, are coated with cinnamon and sugar and dunked into hot chocolate.

What Spanish dessert comes in a pale pink, blue, yellow, or green?

★ *un **pastel*** *(un pastel = pie)*

What did a suspicious Superman say when Lex Luther's Mexican cousin offered him a **thin pancake** for dessert?

★ *"Gracias, but no **crepa** tonight."* *(kryptonite; una crepa = crêpe, thin French pancake)*

> **FUN FACT:** A favorite crêpe in Mexico City is made of corn fungus. It's called a "crepa de huitlacoche." "Huitlacoche" is a fungus known as the "Mexican truffle."

What Spanish Stone Age TV family invented a **custard** dessert?

★ *the **Flan**-stones* *(el flan = Spanish custard with caramel on top)*

> **FUN FACT:** To Spanish-speaking audiences, Fred Flintstone is Pedro Picapiedra (Stonemason) and Barney Rubble is Pablo Mármol (Marble). They live in Bedrock (Piedradura; hard stone).

What American frontiersman from Kentucky opened a Mexican donut shop?

✴ *Daniel **Buñelo*** *(Boone; un buñuelo = deep-fried donut, fritter, or cruller)*

What Mexican pop singer says "oops" when she drops small, puffy deep-fried treats?

✴ *Britney **Sopaipillas*** *(Spears; una sopaipilla = little "pillow" snack covered with cinnamon and sugar or honey)*

What Dr. Seuss book is about a mean Peruvian ogre who lives on a mountain and steals cinnamon sugar-coated chips from the people in the village below?

✴ *"How the Grinch Stole **Crispas"*** *(Christmas; unas crispas = deep-fried tortilla chips coated with cinnamon and sugar)*

FUN FACT: Crispas are really flat sopaipillas made for the fast-food market.

What game are Spanish girls playing when they jump over pieces of **sponge cake**?

✴ *hop **bizcocho*** *(hop scotch; un bizcocho = sponge cake)*

Why did the Mexican who stole the **nougat** get caught so quickly?

✴ *He had nowhere **turrón**. (to run; el turrón = nougat)*

What did Elmer Fudd say to the Spanish **beverage** he was thinking of choosing?

★ *"You could **bebida** one."* *(be the; una bebida = drink)*

> **FUN FACT:** A milkshake is "un batido." Slush is "un granizado." Carbonated water is "agua mineral con gas." In Spain, the cold drink "horchata de chufas," made with tiger nuts, is very popular.

What is the favorite coffee drink of Spanish bullfighting fans?

★ ***café olé*** *(café au lait = coffee with milk; olé = bravo)*

What is the favorite Spanish beverage of a Japanese wrestler?

★ *Sumo de **naranja*** *(un zumo = juice; una naranja = orange)*

SPAIN

★

¡Viva España!

What fabric is used to make workout apparel for Spanish people?

★ **Spain**-*dex (spandex)*

FUN FACT: Spain invented the siesta, gazpacho, sweetened hot chocolate, the novel, the fandango, the guitar, and paella.

What do people from the capital of Spain have in their hair?

★ **Madrid**-*locks (dredlocks; Madrid = capital of Spain since 1562)*

FUN FACT: Madrid is on a plateau 2,000 feet high, almost in the center of the country. Its name comes from the Arabic "Mayrit," based on a word for "source of water." It has an artificial indoor ski slope called the Parque de Nieve Xanadú where people go tubing, skiing, or snowboarding.

What do pilots see when they fly along the Costa del Sol?

★ the **arena** in Spain *(rain; la arena = sand)*

> **FUN FACT:** The Costa del Sol (Sunshine Coast) is a 100-mile stretch of coast in southern Spain. Spain has 3,100 miles of beaches. For almost eleven months of the year, the weather is nice enough for people to go to the beaches.

What was the most popular fast-food chain of the **Moors** in eleventh-century Spain?

★ **árabes** *(Arby's; los árabes = Moors from Africa who ruled Spain from 711 to 1492)*

> **FUN FACT:** The Moors brought mosaics, rice, oranges, dates, cotton, lemons, saffron, artichokes, almonds, apricots, pepper, math, nutmeg, tomatoes, strawberries, bananas, patios, astronomy, irrigation, paper, and the alphabet to Spain.

What are the winters like in the Spanish town known for its barber?

★ very **Sevilla** *(severe; Sevilla [Seville] = capital of Andalucia [Andalusia])*

> **FUN FACT:** The New World was governed from Sevilla. Christopher Columbus is buried there. In *The Barber of Seville*, a French comic opera, sneaky Figaro helps a noble "get the girl."

Who writes parking tickets along the **tree-lined avenues** of Spain?

★ the **alameda** maid *(meter maid; una alameda = tree-lined avenue of Spain)*

What did a mother who lives near the Alhambra palace say as she pointed to her son's very short trousers?

★ "He's **Granada** his pants." *(grown out of; Granada = city in Andalucía [Andalusia])*

FUN FACT: Granada was the last stronghold of the Moors until 1492 when Ferdinand and Isabel defeated them and ended their 800-year rule.

What Spanish dialect is spoken by a romantic Spanish couple when they hug each other?

★ **Catalán** *(cuddlin'; Catalán [Caltalà] = dialect of northeast Spain)*

FUN FACT: Catalán is Spain's second language and is said to look more like French than Spanish. For example, "blau" (blue) is more like the French "bleu" than the Spanish word "azul." Catalán was banned by dictator Francisco Franco for thiry years.

What did the Spanish employee from Catalonia do when his manager's car was getting repaired?

★ He gave his boss a loaner. *(Barcelona = capital of Catalonia)*

FUN FACT: Barcelona, the site of the 1992 Summer Olympics, is a very modern and exciting Mediterranean port and a center of art, fashion, and avant-garde architecture.

What did the Moorish architects in Spain take for indigestion?

★ **Alcazar**-*tzer* *(Alka Seltzer; un alcázar = Arabian palace)*

FUN FACT: Many cities in Spain have an "alcázar" (Spanish spelling) built by the Moors. The most exquisite one is the Alhambra in Granada.

Where do Spanish cheerleaders go to camp to learn cheers for bullfights?

★ *in Pom Pom-plona* (Pamplona = *site of the running of the bulls since 1591*)

FUN FACT: The Fiesta de San Fermín starts at the seventh hour on the seventh day of the seventh month. Thousands run with the bulls for the three-minute, half-mile race in Pamplona.

What did the redneck say when asked where King Ferdinand of Spain was born?

★ *"In Zaragoza, **Aragón**."* (*I reckon;* Aragón = *region in northwest Spain*)

FUN FACT: Aragón is the birthplace of the artist Francisco Goya and of King Ferdinand, who married Isabella of Castile. It's the home of the leaping "jota" dance.

In which Spanish city are stringed instruments played in the streets?

★ *in **Violín**-cia* (Valencia = *third largest Spanish city;* un violín = *violin*)

FUN FACT: Valencia is one of the major growers of oranges and lemons in the world.

What do you call the pride Spanish and Latin American males have in being able to select a good cheddar?

★ *macheesemo* (*cheese;* machismo = *a male attitude about being brave and tough*)

What is a pink Spanish bird with long legs and castanets doing in Andalucía?

★ the **flamenco** *(un flamenco = flamingo; el flamenco = Spanish foot-stomping dance)*

FUN FACT: Flamenco dancing, with the lively guitar, ruffled satin dresses, fancy footwork, and castanet clicking, was born in Andalucía. The fastest flamenco dancer, Solero de Jerez, did sixteen heel taps per second.

What soda causes Spanish men to make **flirtatious comment**s to women?

★ Dr. **Piropo** *(Dr. Pepper; un piropo = flirtatious remark or compliment to a woman)*

FUN FACT: A "piropo" can be very poetic. For example, "Dondequiera que pases, brotan flores" means "Wherever you go, flowers spring up." It can also be a rude comment shouted on the street such as "Oye, bonita," or "Hey, beautiful." Ladies don't respond to "piropos."

What Miguel de Cervantes novel is about the protruding navel of Shrek's sidekick?

★ Donkey Outie *(Don Quixote = Miguel de Cervantes novel from 1605)*

FUN FACT: Don Quixote is an idealistic aristocrat who battles evils on his horse, Rocinante, with his pal, Sancho Panza. He thinks that flocks of sheep are armies and windmills are giants. Cervantes thought "madness is better than a foolish sanity."

What does a Spanish bank teller say to a customer whose check bounces?

★ *"Sorry, but **euro**-ver drawn."* (un euro = Spanish and European currency)

FUN FACT: There are "Todo por un euro" ("Everything's a euro") stores in Madrid. "Lana" (wool) is slang for money in Mexico.

Who do shoppers consult for predictions about the merchandise they'll find at the Madrid **flea market**?

★ a **Rastro**-loger (El Rastro = Madrid's gigantic flea market)

FUN FACT: "El Rastro" is open on the weekends and holidays. It spreads out for many blocks and its vendors sell anything from used clothes to jewelry to knicknacks.

What do Spanish flamenco dancers say they do when they go fishing?

★ *"We cast our nets."* (castanets)

FUN FACT: Castanets (las castañuelas) are small pieces of hollow wood or fiberglass held in each of a flamenco dancer's hands that are clicked together.

What dwarf spins gold and spends time at cafés in Barcelona's mile-long pedestrian district?

★ **Ramblas**-stiltskin (Rumplestiltskin; una rambla = pedestrian avenue)

FUN FACT: Las Ramblas, made up of five streets in a row, is the hippest place to hang out in Barcelona. The area is over a mile long and has shopping, flowers, art, food, cafés, celebrations, street performers, and a party atmosphere.

What Dr. Seuss book is about breakfast at a Spanish palace?

★ Green Eggs and **Alhambra** *(ham; Alhambra = Moorish palace in Granada)*

What do you call a bull from southern Spain that escapes?

★ **andaluz** *(on the loose; andaluz = adjective that means from Andalucía)*

FUN FACT: Andalucía is on the southern coast of Spain. It's famous for bullfighting, flamenco dancing, the Costa del Sol, and castles. From Tarifa it is only twenty miles across the Strait of Gibraltar to Morocco in Africa.

What do people from Don Quixote's homeland call a short relative?

★ a **Mancha**-kin *(Munchkin; Castilla-La Mancha = region in the south of Spain)*

FUN FACT: In La Mancha, tourists can follow the route of Don Quixote to the windmills. The spice saffron comes from La Mancha. The hanging houses of Cuenca balance on cliffs.

What do you get when you cross a Spanish singer and a balloon?

★ **Helio** Iglesias *(Julio; el helio = helium)*

FUN FACT: Julio Iglesias, a former goalie with the Real Madrid professional soccer team, is an international recording artist. His son, Enrique, is a major heartthrob singer, too.

What do Spanish people call it when the Chicago basketball team's offense sprints down the court with the ball?

★ *the running of the Bulls* *(Chicago Bulls; running of the bulls in Pamplona, Spain)*

> **FUN FACT:** Particpants in the popular "encierros" must wear all white with a red scarf or other red item. They are not supposed to get up if they fall.

What is the most famous ice-cream chain in the Spanish Pyrenees?

★ **Basque** *'n Robbins* *(Baskin; Basques = people who live in the Pyrenees)*

> **FUN FACT:** The Basques are a people of mysterious origin, as their language and culture aren't Spanish or French. The beret and pelota (or jai alai) originated in the Basque region.

What character from *The Hobbit* was named after a northern Spanish port?

★ **Bilbao** *Baggins* *(Bilbo; Bilbao = city on the north coast of Spain)*

VEGETABLES

★

Las Legumbres

What did Spanish golfers call it when John swallowed a clove of **garlic**?

★ **ajo** in Juan *(a hole in one; un ajo = clove of garlic)*

FUN FACT: Garlic and olive oil are major ingredients in Spanish cooking. Garlic, along with chile, is also important to Mexican cooking.

What did the Mexican say after eating a three-pound **bean** burrito?

★ *"I can't believe I ate the **frijol** thing."* *(whole; un frijol = bean)*

FUN FACT: According to *Guinness World Records*, the biggest burrito was 3,578 feet long. It was made in 1997 at Burrito Real in Mountain View, California.

What do you call a Spanish **celery** stalk that always thinks it's sick?

★ an **apio**-chondriac *(hypochondriac; un apio = celery)*

What is the name of the Mexican **cucumber** that grew whenever it lied?

★ **Pepino**cchio *(Pinocchio; un pepino = cucumber)*

What did the Mexican farmer say when his baby male **onion** was born?

★ "It's **cebolla**." *(a boy; una cebolla = onion)*

What red vegetable do Spanish people bang on?

★ a tom **tom-ate** *(tom-tom; un tomate = tomato)*

FUN FACT: Buñol, Aragón, celebrates the wild "La Tomatina" festival, which is a giant tomato fight. Over a hundred thousand tons of tomatoes arrive in big trucks. Tens of thousands of people keep shouting, "To-ma-te." Then the truck drivers start hurling tomatoes at the crowd and the fun begins.

What is it called when two Spanish **cabbage**s run into each other?

★ a **col**-lision *(collision; una col = cabbage [Spain])*

What was the favorite sandwich of Inca Indian children?

⋆ *peanut butter and* **chile** *(jelly; un chile = pepper)*

> **FUN FACT:** The Inca Indians believed chile pods contained the knowledge of their ancestors and had magical powers. The pepper was put in all foods and used as money.

Inca Indian children ate peanut butter and chile sandwiches.

Which Spanish magician could make a **green bean** disappear?

⋆ **Judía**-ni *(Houdini; una judía = green bean)*

What green Spanish vegetable was named after the action-hero star of *Die Hard* and *16 Blocks*?

⋆ *las* **coles** *de Bruce Willis (las coles de Bruselas = Brussels sprouts)*

What song from the Spanish version of *The Lion King* tells gardeners not to have any worries about their **spud**s?

★ *"Hakuna **Patata**"* *(Matata; una patata = potato)*

> **FUN FACT:** The Inca Indians of Peru grew 240 kinds of potatoes. A legend tells of an Indian who tried to catch the gods being romantic. For punishment, he was buried in the ground and turned into a potato with useless eyes all over his body.

In which sport do Mexicans chop avocados with their bare hands?

★ *agua-karate* *(un aguacate = avocado)*

Who orchestrates the planting and harvesting of **corn** crops on Mexican farms?

★ *a **maíz**-tro* *(maestro; el maíz = corn)*

> **FUN FACT:** Corn has been a staple of Mexican food since ancient times. The Maya believed man was created by the gods from sacred corn.

What three ships did Columbus and Bugs Bunny's Spanish ancestor sail to the New World?

★ *the Niña, the Pinta, and the **Zanahoria*** *(Santa María; una zanahoria = carrot)*

Why did the **olive** get voted off Spain's version of "American Idol"?

★ *Because it sang out of* **aceituna**. *(tune; una aceituna = olive)*

FUN FACT: Spain's version of "American Idol" is called "Operación Triunfo."

What Spanish vegetable freshens your mouth?

★ *las es-Binacas (Binaca; las espinacas = spinach)*

What did the Spanish woman on the TV game show answer when asked if she could identify the green vegetable in a picture?

★ *"I don't know, but it* **berza** *resemblance to a cabbage."* *(una berza = cabbage)*

What do Spanish dwarfs who sell **garlic** sing on their way to the market each morning?

★ *"**Ajo**, ajo, it's off to work I go."* *(el ajo = garlic)*

What New Mexican Indian tribe grows **turnip**s?

★ *the **Nabo**-jos (Navajos; un nabo = turnip)*

FUN FACT: Salvador Dalí supposedly pulled up to an exhibit in a limousine that was packed with turnips.

What do you call the welcome wreaths made of **beans** that Mexicans put around tourists' necks when they arrive?

★ *frijo-leis* *(leis; los frijoles = beans)*

What brand of diapers do Spanish baby peas wear?

★ *Huggie-santes* *(Huggies; los guisantes = peas)*

What is Señor **Potato**head's favorite kind of pizza?

★ **Papa** *John's* *(una papa = potato)*

 FUN FACT: Indians of Mexico put potato slices on their foreheads for headache pain and used potatoes to cure rashes and pimples.

Why do Mexican fungi eat Wheaties for breakfast?

★ *Because it's the "Breakfast of **Champiñones**." (un champiñón = mushroom)*

What happens to Spanish couples when **rice** is thrown at them at their weddings?

★ *They are **arroz**-ted. (arrested; el arroz = rice)*

 FUN FACT: "Horchata" is a Mexican drink of rice, water, sugar, and cinnamon. "Ser como arroz blanco" ("to be like white rice") in Latin America means to be everywhere.

What does a Mexican **broccoli** grower tell an actor that's about to go onstage?

★ *"**Brécol** leg." (Break a leg; el brécol = broccoli)*

What book do you get when you cross Sherlock Holmes with a Mexican **pumpkin**?

★ The Hound of the **Calabaza**-kervilles *(Baskervilles; una calabaza = pumpkin)*

FUN FACT: "¿Qué te pasa, calabaza?", which means "What's going on, pumpkin?", is a fun greeting in Mexico. The response is "Nada, nada, limonada," or "Nothing, nothing, lemonade."

Spanish vampires are allergic to what Internet search engine?

★ Y-**ajo** *(Yahoo; un ajo = garlic)*

What did the Mexican woman tell her friend when the produce vendor charged four times the usual price for **radishes**?

★ "He's **rábanos** blind." *(robbing us; unos rábanos — radishes)*

¡HASTA LA RISA, BABY!

(LA RISA = LAUGHTER)

(ROUGH TRANSLATION: KEEP SMILING AND LAUGHING!)

EL FIN